ABOUT THE AUTHOR

Jan Kersschot studied medicine at Antwerp University and has practised natural medicine in Belgium since 1986. At the age of seven, questions such as, 'what would it be like if I wasn't here?' were the first appearances of what would be a quest for ultimate truth. His continuing interest in spirituality and philosophy led him to Eastern traditions including Zen Buddhism, Tantra and Advaita Vedanta. Looking for the core of Eastern wisdom and at the same time blending it with a Western lifestyle has been one of the cornerstones of his spiritual search. Meeting Tony Parsons finally led to the end of that search.

This Is It

Dialogues on the Nature of Oneness

JAN KERSSCHOT

INCLUDING INTERVIEWS WITH
ECKHART TOLLE, U.G. KRISHNAMURTI
AND TONY PARSONS

WATKINS PUBLISHING
LONDON

This edition published in the UK in 2004 by
Watkins Publishing, Sixth Floor, Castle House, 75-76 Wells Street,
London W1T 3QH

© Jan Kersschot 2004

Designed and typeset by Jerry Goldie

Printed and bound in Great Britain

British Library Cataloguing in Publication data available

Library of Congress Cataloging in Publication data available

ISBN 1 84293 093 1

www.watkinspublishing.com

There is no path to Being,
Being is the path.
When Being sees Itself,
there is only clear presence.

No matter what you hope 'It' is,
No matter what you imagine 'It' is,
'It' is different from that.

If you are looking for Liberation,
There is some bad news and some good news.
The bad news is that the person you think you are
will never find Liberation.
The good news is that what You really are
is already awakened.

CONTENTS

Foreword by Tony Parsons

This Is It invites the seeker to investigate the possibility that there is no one and nothing that needs to be liberated. The author speaks easily and clearly about moving beyond effort, belief and path into a new perception that sees everything as the expression of wholeness.

Jan Kersschot interviews many communicators in his book, but he is one of the very few who speaks without compromise about the direct perception that is available to all.

TONY PARSONS,
AUTHOR OF *THE OPEN SECRET* AND *AS IT IS*

Preface

This book doesn't offer any form of therapy or healing, nor is it a teaching that suggests that there is a spiritual path leading to enlightenment. The awakening referred to in this book has nothing to do with your personal attributes. So don't expect any exercises or instructions on how to live life, because all prescriptive and goal-oriented approaches only confirm you are a seeker going to a better future.

Most popular teachings about enlightenment are based on the mistaken idea that there is a seeker who will finally attain self-realization. What you might find here is the possibility of withdrawing the belief in the person who sits here reading this book. Just forget about the idea that something spiritual is going to happen to you. Maybe you will also find out that the separate individual you always believed yourself to be is just an idea, a concept in the mind.

When it is clear that the seeker is a ghost, what can you do? Can a concept attain something higher? Does this phantom need any improvement at all? If there is no you, where are you going? Do you believe that a ghost can find Liberation?

JAN KERSSCHOT
MARCH 2004

Introduction

Most books about spirituality and enlightenment deal with personal growth. They suggest that there is a higher goal to be reached; something the sages have attained which you haven't attained (yet). This only confirms your sense of separation. A lot of these books are about 'you' who are supposed to do things in order to become better. They respond to your belief that something is wrong with you, and that you have to work on yourself. These teachings confirm your belief that you have to be more spiritual in order to be open to enlightenment.

All that is very attractive to the mind because these teachings give you hope. Maybe you felt a glimpse of enlightenment and now you want to feel that all the time. Maybe you want to become like your spiritual heroes by imitating them or by doing what they tell you to do. Or your mind can do the opposite: you get disappointed because you realize you will never become as perfect as they seem to be. You realize that you will never 'get it'. Whether you desperately want it or whether you fear you will never make it, both options confirm you are a separate identity. What if the person you think you are is only a concept in the mind?

This book questions the common belief that there is a person reading these words right now; that you are an individual who is standing or sitting here reading this book; that you are a person who is holding this book in his or her hands. The identification with body and mind is very practical for everyday life, but when it comes to Liberation, it is interesting to discover that your personality only exists as a phantom – an idea appearing in the mind. I don't expect you to believe me in this matter, but just consider the possibility of what I am saying and see what happens.[1]

The Liberation I refer to is quite different from the old idea about spiritual enlightenment that is still around: a higher state someone special received because he was chosen by the gods or because he worked so hard on it (for decades or even lives) that he was finally rewarded with the highest prize a human being can ever get. Once attained, this enlightenment is assumed to reflect perfection, peace, goodness and permanent bliss. To me, enlightenment has nothing to do with perfection. It has nothing to do with sitting on a throne. It is not about Jan looking down on other people. It is not about Jan leading his readers to a higher state. The concept of being Jan is just another image appearing in awareness. It has nothing to do with 'me' and still I can say, 'What I really am is life happening. And since nothing can be excluded, everything that appears is what I am. There are no more borders, although there are still concepts about borders appearing in the mind.'

The paradox in this book is of course that it seems to be about me and the people I have met during the interviews (see part three). Don't pay too much attention to my story, or to their stories. Such stories usually focus on the personal aspects and the temporary elements of life, while this book tries to point at that which is impersonal and timeless.

Furthermore, if you focus on the meaning of the words, you may not sense what the words are pointing at. Words are dualistic in nature, and will always fail in describing nondualism. But I have to use words: there is no other way when writing a book. That is why obviously this book is full of inconsistencies and contradictions. It attempts only to point at nondualism – knowing that nondualism can never be pointed at. So it is doomed to fail anyway.

Although I will have to use words like 'you' and 'me' and

'us', it is clear that these only exist as concepts in the mind. In fact, there is no 'me' and no 'you'. You may presume that I am talking to you through these words, but there is no one sitting here reading. The person you think you are is just a concept in the mind, a game of memory which gives it apparently a permanent status. It's a phantom. It is clear that if there is no separate 'you', I can't offer you a lot. What can one phantom give to another phantom? So I can't give you any hope, not because your situation is hopeless but simply because there is no 'you'. So don't expect any strategies or secret paths. Even when sometimes you have the feeling that I suggest you should be or behave in a certain way, read that particular book, go and see a particular teacher or give up whatever you think should be given up, ignore it: there really is nowhere to go. I can't bring you to where you already are. I can't give you your true nature if you are already being it.

The enlightenment this book is trying to point at has nothing to do with your spiritual materialism. Forget about all your ambitions in this matter. If there is no 'you' then where should you go? What is the use of turning a concept into a more holy concept? Even saying 'let it be', 'enquire into the self', 'accept what is', or 'do nothing' is still a subtle way of addressing the individual you think you are. What is the point of suggesting all this if the 'you' isn't even there? If the person is but a concept in the mind, what use is it trying to make it more spiritual? What use is it to become a better phantom? Can an illusion become enlightened?

Reading this book will not give you anything, but it may take away your spiritual ambitions. Not because you have to get rid of them, not because then you can reach something still higher, but simply because there is no 'you' in the first place.

One:

Where are you going?

BEINGNESS

While reading the words on this page, you are conscious of them appearing in your present awareness, aren't you? Maybe you are also aware of certain parts of your body. All these images confirm that you *are*. You can't say, 'I am not'. Experiencing this sense of being is maybe one of the most basic recognitions there is. Just being here, just *being*. Wherever you go, there is this same sense of being. No matter how you feel or what you think, this 'sense of being' is available to you and to everyone.

If you want to take a closer look at this being, or this 'Is-ness,' you may feel a certain discomfort because your mind is not able to grasp Is-ness. The person you think you are will try to lay claim to it but it has nothing to do with you as a person. It has nothing to do with being in a special state of conscious-ness. As soon as you think you get it, it (apparently) escapes. It is like trying to grab a bar of soap in water: the harder you try, the more you fail. At the same time, it is obvious that 'it' is right here. Is-ness cannot escape, and yet you can never practise how to 'just be'. It is impossible because you are already doing it! It is obvious that this sense of being is never far away since it is witnessing your thoughts and emotions. So, it must be right 'here'. Being is the closest you can get and still the mind fails to get hold of it. That is the paradox. How can something be so present and available and yet be incomprehensible for the mind?

Maybe you will see that this being is not a personal thing but that it's borderless. Where does being stop? Nobody can tell you where it ends. If it has no borders, if it's limitless, there can't be two of them; it is all-encompassing. We could call it Unicity because there is only one of it and it can't be cut into pieces. And the term Unicity is given a capital to emphasize its limitless nature: it encompasses everything that is witnessed. Although it is indescribable, you can give it any name you wish, like Awareness, Is-ness, Consciousness, the Unknown, the Source, Light or Presence. This is the *Witness* of Advaita, the *Original face* according to Zen, the *Father* of Christianity, the *Buddha-mind* of the Chinese Ch'an. Some call it Shiva, Brahman, Nirvana, God or Spirit. In this book, the word *Beingness* is used mostly because it sounds neutral. Other terms used here are Oneness, Life, Unicity, Silence, Space and It.[2] In the end, the names or descriptions you use don't matter that much. Some terms however – especially the religious ones – can be quite confusing because then the mind may imagine it can put It into a specific frame and then take hold of It. Or you may believe you know what you are talking about because you know the meaning of the words. However, your brain and senses can't observe this Awareness, it is rather Awareness seeing Awareness. Light recognizing Light. Life mirroring Life. Is-ness seeing Is-ness. And Is-ness is all there is. There is nothing outside of it.

When you recognize that you inherently *are* this endless Beingness, that you *are* this Space without boundaries, the struggle to find or even feel Beingness ceases automatically. Where should you go to find It if It is everywhere? And realizing that, there is no longer a sense that you should be different from what you are in the present moment. There is also less investment in guilt and regret, and also less dependence on hope or purpose. It is the end of the subject–object relationship. It is the end of believing you are a seeker who has to attain a higher state.

Losing conditioning and beliefs lets life flow naturally. The sense of individual doership falls away. Still, things are (apparently) being done. Like a mountain river, the water just flows. When a stone is encountered on the path, the water just goes around it and continues on its way. Everything is allowed to take its course, although there is no active process of allowing going on. You could say that on the spiritual level, nothing matters anymore,[3] and yet there is no sense of detachment or indifference. It is just clear that there is nothing spiritual or religious that has to be done in order to express Is-ness, and at the same time everything is possible. Nothing is excluded. Everything (and everyone) can be as it is. That may sound like infinite freedom, but there is no person who can lay claim to this freedom. There is no more attachment to spiritual expectations or religious moral codes. When Oneness is seen, all these games of the seeking mind are seen as side issues. Everything is allowed to go its way, and it is recognized that this has been happening all along. Everything is already taking its course.

Looking for Oneness is not like a puzzle you have to solve, in which you take all the different pieces and try to figure it out. It is just the opposite. The basic understanding is that the 'you' who needs to work it out is a phantom. When the central position of the 'you' is abandoned, there is just a gentle OK-ness, a liquid witnessing of what appears in life. When you recognize your true nature as Beingness, when Oneness is seen as all there is, there may be a fluid adaptability because the investment in a personal agenda becomes less important. The more this Beingness is recognized for what it is, the more you realize how ordinary it is to just *be*. It is not you recognizing Beingness, it is not a personal achievement, it is not a gradual process you have to go through, it is just Being recognizing Being. The 'me' you usually believe you are just can't manage it. It's simply about being without any sense that things could have been any different from how they are. It's as simple as that. You don't have to still the mind for that because you are stillness itself. And this stillness allows all sorts of noises of the mind to appear in it, similar to space letting all sorts of objects appear in it.

WINDOWS TO BEINGNESS

The way Beingness is expressed seems unique for each individual. Everything you think or feel or do is conditioned by your genetic code and your personal programming, and that is how it is. On the human level, we all appear to be unique expressions of Oneness. This uniqueness is not just there in the daydream, but also in the (apparent) process of waking up. A seeker who reports a transcendental happening usually turns it into a personal experience. When you actually believe you have had an awakening experience you come up with an individual story, and the mind can get easily excited by that. But each report of a personal Liberation is only another part of the daydream. Beingness itself cannot be described or experienced. Such happenings can be *windows* into Beingness, like the sudden appearance of a white page in a book, or a white screen in the middle of a film. It is like Light seeing Light. When the images start to appear again, the mind comes in and starts to talk about what happened. The ego wants to understand. The seeker wants to claim 'it' as a personal achievement. The mind wants to own the white screen. The person wants to be a pure reflection of the Light. All these tricks of the mind only perpetuate the spiritual search.

Some masters report that they have come home to their true nature. There are many books in which you can find what people describe as (their) awakening. In most cases, the story is presented as a personal achievement. However, some of them have realized that this awakening has nothing to do with their person.

The realization of one's true nature may come to the surface in many ways, but it is important to notice that the way it appears has no significance at all. There are no standard procedures. Some already live in the light, and just go (apparently) from light to an ever bigger light. Very smoothly – without anyone noticing it – they seem to disappear into Beingness. They usually don't report a major awakening experience.

Some seekers have been in misery and depression for several decades. When they discover the light, the change can be so huge that they can have a major awakening event. That may be very blissful and peaceful – imagine how it is to strike a match in a cellar if you haven't seen daylight for several decades – but the trap is that the first impact of that light is now considered as the standard of how one should feel all the time. You may believe you found it and then lost it again. In that case, you can chase that feeling of peace and bliss for the rest of your life. Although there is nothing wrong with that, although it is still an equal expression of Beingness, you are back in the horse race.[4]

Some seekers have been looking for the Holy Grail for several decades. When all the burdens of the desperate seeking are finally dropped, the leap may be so huge that indeed it may come to the surface as a spectacular event, as a big relief. Such experiences can be very inspiring but can also be misleading. You can mislead yourself (and others) by presenting your awakening experience as the standard to look for.

You can also mislead yourself by comparing yourself with others. Reading about other seekers' testimonies of what they call their awakening can be very confusing. It can easily become frustrating when you imagine you are not there yet as you compare your own experience (or the lack of it) with the experience described by someone else. When the awakening event is personalized, your mind turns it into an experience. As a result, it is claimed as a personal reward the seeker has attained at a certain point of time, and if the awakening continues to be there for the mind, the seeker may believe he or she is actually awakened and has attained real enlightenment, not realizing that Enlightenment cannot be achieved by a person. Even a transcendental experience can't bring you any closer to Beingness.

Still, transcendental happenings can be very inspiring indeed. Such events can unmask the belief in your personal story. It is the belief in being a seeker (or being an experiencer) that seems to overshadow the recognition of Unicity. When that belief suddenly drops away, there simply is 'what is' without any sense that things should be different from how they are.

Maybe you recognize the impersonal aspect of Beingness while you are outside in a natural environment, seeing that all boundaries are gone and that there is no separate you to recognize it. Everything is just as it is. The natural elements are good examples of Beingness that don't pretend to have the ability to be other than what they are. Your mind can't grasp it and uses words like emptiness or wholeness; this is simply infinity seeing infinity. Maybe you recognize this wholeness during a blissful moment while meditating or while making love: suddenly there is a sense of clear emptiness and nobody being there to witness this emptiness.

Some people report opening to this wholeness while being with their spiritual master. Or maybe there is a recognition that the seeker is a concept without ever having had a mystical experience at all. However, if there is still in the back of your mind a gentle whisper that it is *you* who will be awakened, you will only be disappointed. There is simply nothing to chase, no hero to be imitated, nowhere to go. And why is that? Because the 'separate you' who does the chasing or imitating is conceptual. One of the tricks of the mind is to suggest that there is a separate you who can prepare for enlightenment, that you can actually attain enlightenment while others are still unenlightened. That is one of the many traps around. The belief in a personal Liberation is not bringing you closer to the Awakening referred to in this book. This Awakening is impersonal. It is the natural way of being, and natural can mean just anything here.

Both transcendental happenings as well as flashes of intuitive insight are irresistibly compelling for the seeking mind because they often seem to function as 'windows' into Beingness. This is why they can have such a profound impact upon you, and why you feel drawn toward a deepening of this recognition, but that is exactly where the mind comes in and wants to turn this into a process again. Finally you will have to forget about holy rituals, wise action, trying to be spiritual and all the rest. There are no steps or rules to attain Liberation. Where you are right now, that is exactly where you are supposed to be. How you are, is exactly how you are supposed to be. Even if you don't feel blissful or peaceful right now; even when you think you are still in the horse race.

Once you focus on blissful states, it only creates more

separation between you and Beingness, or between the apparent you and the apparent others. All of it is just another expression of dualism. The same goes for the spiritual level of the guru. Your mind imagines that there is a border between you and the sage, but Beingness has no borders because there is only one of it. So Beingness doesn't have any hierarchy! You are invited to forget about all the spiritual heroes you heard of, and to ignore all the dogmatic teachings of the religious leaders you have read about. You are also invited to forget about the concept you have about yourself. Whether you think you are a loser or a winner is not relevant here. Even a neurosis and a depression are not able to take away Beingness. Even being peaceful and feeling at one with everything is not bringing you closer to Is-ness. Even 'spiritual experiences' are just images appearing, but these are not the Light itself. These images are not yours, even the concepts you have about yourself aren't yours, because the person you think you are is also an image passing by. Even the most blissful experiences you ever had aren't yours. Even your dark night of the soul isn't yours. And the same goes for 'your' pain, 'your' joy or 'your' bliss.[5] They are happenings rather than experiences. Even 'your' transcendental experiences are but images passing by. Some of them seem to be very personal, but in the end they are not yours.

What you *think* you are is just a role you play, but what you really are is That in which all these experiences (including your character) are appearing. And That is not a special state, it is not something you can experience or see, it is what you *are*. It is the Light in the images of the film you believe you are playing in. So you will never experience Oneness – there *is* only Oneness. You will never attain enlightenment, there is only Light. All 'your' experiences – from sitting in a bus to the highest state of consciousness – are the content of Awareness, not Awareness itself.

The recognition of Beingness may (or may not) influence your concepts and belief systems. You may realize that all your thoughts and perceptions are just ripples on the surface of the ocean. After Oneness is seen, the need to look for a spiritual goal is gone, the desire to imitate your spiritual heroes has vanished. It becomes ridiculous to compare yourself with others because it is seen that comparing is also a conceptual game. As a result, all your spiritual frustrations, all your religious pride and seriousness melt away. All the old thought patterns are now seen in a different perspective. You may realize that some spiritual teachers gave you more concepts about what you are, and added more concepts about how you should be. Being fascinated by all these concepts and belief systems, you added more weight to your precious collection of spiritual achievements. Stimulated by the belief you can reach a higher goal in the future, you tried to become more holy, more radiant, more peaceful, more intelligent, more spiritual, and tried to get rid of your bad habits or your bad karma. One day you see it is all about yourself. You are only playing an egocentric game. All this seeking is finally about your 'me' trying to become better, to be in a higher state. But the 'me' you think you are is just a ghost. It is just an actor playing in a movie.[6] When the 'me' is unmasked, where is there to go?

The daydream is the common idea that you are a separate person living in that body, and that the others are living in bodies, too. But as said before, nobody ever found this person. When the separate you is recognized as a construction of the mind, the spiritual seeking is over, and automatically all the importance you gave to your religious growth is over. The 'normal' everyday life habits seem to go on, but all the ritualistic, hierarchical and dogmatic aspects of formal religion lose their importance when it is clear that it is all part of a conceptual game. You were only trying to feed your own materialism

– no matter if it was through devotion, altruism, prayer, discipline or understanding. This doesn't mean that now you are going to criticize these organizations, or try and convince their followers that they are wrong and you are right, because that too would be a struggle with what is. What happens is that all your religious ambitions lose their impact on you. They are like toys you used to play with as a child. The whole game of trying to be more awake has simply been seen through. In a way, the old magic of following a path or imitating a spiritual hero is gone, and that may feel like you lost something, but what you've lost was only another construction of the mind. When all the spiritual authorities and traditions are put aside, you can just *be*. Just be in all simplicity without any plans, formulas or answers.

TEACHERS OF NONDUALISM

The teacher you are attracted to is just a reflection of what you are looking for. If you had a major transcendental experience while being with a particular guru, you are likely to get hooked on that teacher, or hooked on such an experience. And if that teacher is not satisfying any more, you may go and look for a stronger or more resonating leader. As long as you are looking for something, be it bliss, resonance or peace, you will encounter teachers or masters who will claim that they can give it to you. As long as this process is going on, it is OK to follow them. It is also OK to have spiritual experiences, and to look for more of those until there is the recognition that the 'final it' is not attained yet – and never will be. Until it is recognized that blissful experiences are appearing in It but are *not* It, it seems that all this seeking and all these special experiences can bring you closer, but not close enough.

Other teachers may look more ordinary, and focus on the

intellectual approach of the spiritual search. They can challenge some of your belief systems. Finally, one can encounter someone who leaves you with nothing whatsoever.[7] No prescriptive measure is given since it is made clear that there is no such thing as a spiritual path. There are only a few around who don't compromise in this matter, who continue to say that there is nothing to chase because there is no spiritual seeker in the first place. Here the seeker's mind may be disappointed because there is no more hope, no more future. Even special experiences are not considered important any more. Even your most extraordinary spiritual achievements are not encouraged nor labelled as higher or more profound than your most ordinary sense of everyday life. Even comparing yourself with the teacher falls away. This is the teacher who gives no basis for a maintenance of your personality. Then all that is left is presence. It becomes clear that searching for something special or trying to be peaceful and openhearted doesn't bring you closer to the very natural state you are always in, no matter how you feel or behave. Beingness is not something you can acquire as a result of your personal effort. The actor on the movie screen isn't able to walk up to the lamp in the back of the theatre. Nobody can bring you closer to the Light and nothing can take you away from It because Light is what you are. Beingness is what you are. And this Being is completely beyond any sense of values.

When all beliefs and expectations are abandoned, all the usual efforts to improve your life or to achieve a higher level of consciousness evaporate. When the spiritual search is no longer important, there may be a resting in the immediacy of what is. Seeking the extraordinary, you overlook the splendour of the ordinary in everyday life. You overlook the simplicity of the open secret, which is available right here and right now. Enlightenment is not something you can reach and that will make you special, something that will make you stand out in the crowd. It is just the opposite: you become nobody and everybody at the same time.

ORDINARY AWARENESS

All this comes down to is *ordinary present awareness*. It is as simple as that: the awareness that allows you to read these words right now, that's it. That is really it! It is the same awareness that is glimpsed in your most spectacular mystical experience. It is the same awareness as the avatars and sages 'have'. The reason why I can say so without proving it is that this awareness is limitless, borderless, and as a result there is only one awareness. That's why 'your' awareness equals *the* Awareness. No need to look any further.

So if there is only one and it's limitless, nobody can be excluded. The Beingness I refer to in this book is not a personal thing, and as a result It can't be limited to an exceptional few. It's not something I have and you don't have. It is not something 'out there'.

This book may help to break up many of the myths some spiritual seekers still have about enlightenment and their admiration of the 'awakened ones'. Liberation is just a matter of melting into what is, leaving behind the usual stories and beliefs about awakening. So really one doesn't awake, one simply stops pretending to be a separate person who needs to advance on the spiritual level. We are the Light, and the person we identify with is just another role the Light seems to play. And once it is seen that all the various costumes people put on are but temporary roles, it doesn't matter anymore what kind of costume you are wearing. It is clear then that there is no need to change anything whatsoever in your play. The Light doesn't care anyway. And that doesn't mean that you will lose your sense of responsibility, respect or compassion for others after reading this book. Although there are no strict rules, most people who see what this book is about come to a natural respect and compassion for others, not because their religious codes tell them to take care of others but because it is clear that there is only one Awareness and that we are all That.

The Liberation I am referring to is not something I have attained or even glimpsed, it is That in which the concepts about Jan's life are appearing. It is the infinite Space in which the images of 'getting enlightened' or 'not getting it' are appearing. One could say that when the belief in the apparent separate person drops away, the presence of Oneness becomes clear and obvious. Sometimes that recognition can be very spectacular, but not necessarily so. Many seekers have reported similar 'experiences', but most of them don't realize it happened to nobody. So if I talk about Liberation, it didn't become clear and obvious to Jan but rather to Itself. The paradox is that it seemed to become clear to me *while I wasn't there*. That seemed to bring the spiritual search to an end. When that became clear, it was also obvious that the person I believed I was, is purely conceptual and always has been – although there is still on the screen the appearance of individuality for purely practical reasons. There is nothing wrong with the concept of being an individual appearing and disappearing.[8] It is simply part of life happening. It's part of the opera. Both identification as well as non-identification are allowed to appear. The Jan I usually believe I am is not in charge. It is just an image appearing on the screen. Whether this image still appears on the screen or not is absolutely not relevant at all. The Light doesn't even know about Jan and all the others, the Light just shines. And that Light is what I really am.

There is only one player in this play, and that one player is doing it all. Even when the appearances of everyday life suggest that we are all separate doers and creators, there is only one Presence, one Beingness. And when you look at your own experience right now, there is already Presence available in its full glory. Nothing is lacking! And that can go with a sense of being open and feeling unlimited, but not necessarily so. Such a sense may even be confusing for the mind because the mind will associate a sense of peace and openness with being enlightened. Anyway, there is already Awareness here, and you don't have to do anything for that. When this is understood, it is obvious that it is unnecessary (and impossible) to improve Beingness in any way at all. There is nothing you can do for or against It, there is nothing you can do with It and nothing you can do without It. How could the actor on the screen ever be able to improve the Light?

The Light is so available and at the same time nobody notices It. Nobody ever notices It because Beingness cannot be noticed or recognized. It is closer than you can imagine since It is what you are. At the same time, It is reflected everywhere. That is the open secret. So, the personal life story goes on, the role you play is not interrupted but there is less personal engagement in the individual role because the rigid belief in your life story falls away. The movie of your life goes on, but you know that you aren't a character, you are the Light, and the Light has no borders, which means it is reflected everywhere. When I say everywhere I really mean everywhere: nothing or nobody is excluded. When that is clear, there is truly nowhere to go, no more seeking approval, nothing to attain, nothing 'higher' to hope for. Now you may stop believing that Liberation is all about 'you'. Once the whole game of the mind is seen through, there is no way back. Then there is just *this*, just Presence. Just Beingness.

Two:

Let It Be

FROM OPENNESS TO IDENTIFICATION

As newborns, all we are is open attention. There is absolutely no sense of separation. There is just limitlessness. There isn't even the idea of being a baby lying in a bed. We don't know yet about our sex, name, nationality or characteristics. There is absolutely no sense of the 'me' as an individual entity.[9] All there is is presence. We don't believe yet that we are living in a particular body, although it looks like that to our parents. There is also no sense of past or future, and no sense of right or wrong. There is just being. All there is is clear openness, borderless attention.[10]

Our parents give us a name when we are born, but it takes a while before we accept that name as our identity. It also takes a few years before we accept that we are a person. At some point – usually around the age of two or three – the belief in being limited to this particular body takes over. That is where the original Oneness[11] gets lost. We are all invited to play the game of becoming a separate person. That is the ticket we need to join the club of adults. And that sense of being limited gradually takes over our original sense of being limitless. It starts by making the distinction between our body and the rest

of the world: my arm, my toe, and so on. This process of identification expands further to feelings of hunger, pain, joy, and
so on. The mind will stimulate this process by using language,
memory and abstraction. And so we say, 'my body, my clothes,
my toy, my candy'. So we go (apparently) from openness to
identification, from limitlessness to separation, from nondualism
to dualism. We learn from our parents that there is 'me' and
'the others'. That sense of separation is continued while we
grow up, and we add ever new concepts which confirm this
game. The 'me' who is claiming all these deeds and thoughts is
becoming like a substantial entity, with a body and mind; a
personality with characteristics, a history and free will.

The sense of separation is essential for adult life, of course.
That is how society works. Language will confirm again and
again that we are limited to this body and mind. And since
everybody else seems to believe the same thing, we feel
comforted by the idea of being separate, too. We give up our
openness and join the club of the grown-ups. That is where
paradise is lost. The intelligence of the mind takes over and the
brilliance and openness of our original nature is (seems to be)
lost.

The rest of our adult life usually comes down to making
our lives work. We have a body to take care of, and a mind to
control what we think and do. We are told that we have free
will, the choice between good and evil, and we get a list of
what we should do and what we should avoid. Not only do
we receive a character, we also get a role to play, and the strong
suggestion that we have to play our role as well as we can. The
question is now: what if the above story is based on a fallacy?
What is the point of making our life work if the character is just
a role? If the person we believe we are is only a ghost?

THREE MAJOR BELIEF SYSTEMS

There are three major belief systems which keep us going in the spiritual search. The first one is the concept of being an individual. This belief leads to the separation between me and the others. The second one is the concept of there being a time axis: this leads to the division between past and future. The third one is the division of the world into high and low, into holy and evil. It originates from our need to divide things and people into good and bad, into spiritual and not spiritual, into samsara and nirvana.

1. separation between me and the others
2. division between past and a future
3. division of the world into high and low

All three of them cut Oneness into two (dualism). Practical as these three belief systems may seem in everyday life, each one is completely conceptual. All three are essential for the personality to survive as a ghost, they seem to be essential for the functioning of society, but when we want to point at nondualism we will have to question all three of them.

It is clear that these three belief systems are essential to build up a personal story with expectations, fears and hopes. They are the basic elements required to create the role we play in our opera. They are essential to keep us on the spiritual path. But when we take a closer look at them, are these belief systems still as solid as they always seemed to be?

One of the great contexts in which society seems to live is the belief in the separate identity (1). The habit of believing in a separate person is so strong, and passed on from generation to generation, that hardly anyone questions its validity. However, when we take a closer look at this personality, it becomes very difficult to catch it. Nobody seems to be able to find this person inside.[12] We only know it as a concept in the mind! The question is now, 'How can we be this personality if this image of being a person is just a concept appearing in our mind a few times a day?' Is that what we really are: an idea that we pick up from memory? Or is what we are something that doesn't come and go? Is our true nature something that goes beyond the image of being limited to a personal identity?

Equally important – and strongly related to the first context – is the use of a time frame (2). It is another great tool which confirms our sense of separation. What would our personality be worth if it had no history? What is left of us when we can't consider our (personal) past? Who would we be if we had no deeds or memories to reflect upon, or no better future to hope for? The sense of past and future is another essential element in the maintenance of the conceptual world.[13]

The third belief is closely related to the other two: the division between holy and evil (3). Cutting the world into spiritual and profane, into high and low, into nirvana and samsara is another game of the mind. The world itself doesn't even know about these, it is just a concept in the mind of certain people. Where is the border between spiritual and profane? As a result, we understand the saying of Buddha, 'Samsara is nirvana, nirvana is samsara – they are not two.' Dividing the world into good versus evil is a very strong frame of humanity that fascinates us and drives us. Dividing the people around us into the good guys and the bad guys is a very popular game of the mind.

GOOD AND EVIL

In this book, these three belief systems will be put into perspective because that may bring new light to misconceptions and veils in the spiritual field.[14] Let us have a closer look at the last one first. The third belief system separates high from low (3). What would happen if we see that the division between holy and evil is purely conceptual? What does it mean if good and bad are but concepts in our mind? And what is the point of suggesting that holy and evil are balanced like left and right?

A lot of people worry about the idea that there is no such thing as good or bad on the spiritual level, because it could mean that we lose our moral codes. They might get angry because they strongly feel that it would be the end of morality and justice. As a result, they can't accept that good and bad are relative terms, only existing in the heads of those persons who believe in that particular system. Although they know that each religion has different codes, they hold onto their own belief system and they are willing to protect it with any means. They are worried about what would happen if all of us unmasked the belief system concerning right and wrong. If we all believed what this book postulates, what would happen to our sense of responsibility? If people agreed that there is no evil, where would that lead us to? If we say that there is no good without bad but in our minds maybe we would all become indifferent. What would happen to our ability to love and help each other? Maybe we would all become terrorists.

It is true that we need rules to organize everyday life. So there is definitely a sense of good versus bad when it comes to stopping for a red traffic light, for example. This book is not attacking the rules of society. All the practical codes have their value when it comes to running life smoothly. The sense of good versus bad can have value on that level, but when it comes to Liberation, we see that all these divisions only create confusion. All the moral codes from the spiritual traditions create a veil which seems to cover Oneness. Good and bad are not in the objects or persons we observe, they appear in our own minds, and we project these onto that object, situation or person.

It is clear that moral codes allow us to judge and criticize others. The division between holy and evil also gives us good reasons to fight 'evil' with all means. But fighting against evil is also a fight. The history of the last 2,000 years shows us that such a fight against evil can appear on many levels and in many different ways, from organizing the Crusades to walking into a restaurant or train with a bomb.

Still, it is believed that fighting what is wrong is good for us and for the world. As a result, those who suggest that there is no right or wrong appear to be a danger for society. However, realizing that holy and evil are but ideas in our minds doesn't turn us into terrorists. Quite the contrary: most terrorists seem to act from a strong sense of 'working towards a better world' by fighting the evil forces they believe are around. The fundamentalists of each religion have their own standards, and at some point they will encounter the fundamentalists of another belief. Each group believes that they are the good guys and the others the bad guys. Both of them have a strong sense that the others (the bad guys) must be punished or killed. Since each group has its own moral codes and its own sense of what is evil, and both groups believe their system is the best one, they will both do all they can to protect their own interests.

Although we can all sense that there is indeed no good without bad because we fabricate them in the mind, we still seem to feel the need to stimulate or reward the ones we believe are good and fight or punish the ones we believe are bad. But does it really work that way? Can we influence the balance of right and wrong? Can we put light on the front of an object without creating a shadow on the back? What if good and bad are always balanced by each other, just like north pole and south pole? What if holy and evil are always compensating each other, just like left and right? If that were true, all our attempts to work for a better world would become useless.[15] It is not easy to prove this, but if one compensated for the other it would be ridiculous even to try and manipulate the world. Trying to work towards Utopia is like wanting to have a landscape with more mountains – but *not* with more valleys. Maybe we would find out it is just like moving the furniture around. Trying to turn the universe into a better place is like hoping for a battery with only a positive pole. And this is also true for the spiritual quest: can we really work on a better future? There are always two sides to a coin.[16] Maybe the back of the coin will also grow while we are working on the front.

PAST AND FUTURE

The second belief system concerns the existence of past and future (2) – the concept of time that keeps us reflecting on the past and projecting a future more or less based on our personal history. Our sense of a personal past is like our footprints in sand: they only exist in as far as we look back and remember them, but looking back at our footprints is also happening in the present moment. Although these footprints seem to be distinct, they are indistinguishable from the substance of what surrounds them. The borders are only in the mind. The question is if time really exists outside the web of conceptualization. Can we perceive the past? Is there anyone who has ever lived one minute in the future? Perceptions, thoughts and feelings come to the surface, seem to stay for a split second and then disappear. This sequence of events is construed by the mind (by memory) as past, present and future. Similar to the images appearing on a white screen, the movie seems to pass through the present, but if we want to take hold of the present, we can't. We could say there is only now, but where is this 'now'? Even the present moment, even the 'now' is a concept of the mind. All we can say is that all thoughts and concepts arise and disappear in the same timelessness.

ME AND OTHERS

Now let us have a look at the first belief system, the sense of feeling separate from other people (1). This belief system, which is programmed very strongly, concerns our sense of being a doer. It is related to our habit of identifying with our body and mind. It is connected to our sense of feeling separate from the rest of the human population, to our sense of having free will. In the role we play, each moment is unique and has never happened before. The past and future are concepts of the ego that keep us locked in the role that we think we play. Memory and projection are essential parts to make our story look real, and so are all the feelings and characteristics we think we own. We have learned to identify with the characteristics that we are told to have, but is that what we really are: a collection of thoughts, characteristics and memories? They just appear and disappear, and they seem to be very personal, but who says that they are ours? Where is this person who claims to be the doer? Does this person really exist or is it an image in our brain?

When we simply become aware of whatever is happening in the present moment and we don't pay attention to the inner voice that suggests that there is a person sitting here watching, it may become clear that all there is is present moment awareness. All there is is Beingness in which everything is appearing. The person we think we are is just the main character in 'our' movie. Although this role we play seems to be real, although our senses confirm that we seem to be living inside this body, could it be that identifying with this character is just a habit we took over from our parents? Is it no more than an educational programme we received in order to be able to function in society? If we take a closer look at this character, we could say it is an image in our movie. Although it is labelled as the main character, it is but an image which appears now and then on the screen.[17] Is that what we are: an image that appears temporarily on a screen? However, the light which lets our movie shine is available 'all the time'. Is it possible that we are the light instead of the character? Is what we really are an image on the screen that appears on a regular basis, or is it that which is always available?

WHO CHOOSES?

Strongly related to our belief in being a separate identity is our sense of having free will. There are two popular theories in philosophy regarding the existence of *free choice*: the theory of different futures spreading out from the present, depending on our own decisions, and the theory that says everything is programmed and our life is like a celluloid movie that we are witnessing. The first theory accepts the existence of free will and the second is based on predestination. The differences between them are obvious. One starts from the belief that there is a person who decides, who can manage his or her thoughts and deeds. This is the most popular vision around: it says we can choose, it postulates that we can control our lives.

According to the second theory, there is no way that we can escape our conditioning. Predestination means that our future is fixed, we are not able to decide what we think or do and can only act as programmed. Our life is like a videotape, and there is nothing we can do about what happens in our movie. Those who believe there is no such thing as free choice say, 'If we really can decide what we think and do, why do we continue to have all these conflicts, all these depressions, all these problems?' They argue, 'If you believe you are able to choose your own thoughts, why don't you decide right now to have only nice and happy thoughts for the rest of your life?'

When we take a closer look at our so-called decisions, we may notice that our decisions also come out of our programming. They are but responses, conditioned by past experiences, warnings, social habits and so on. They are based on instinct, memory and education. So even when we feel that we can choose and decide, maybe we only *believe* we can. We imagine we are thinking our own thoughts, but we are only witnessing what comes up in our minds. Even claiming that the thoughts coming up in 'our' brain are *our* thoughts – that we choose them or engineer them ourselves – is again another idea coming to the surface as an image on the screen.

To some people it can be liberating to see that we can't control life. Realizing that we don't manage our thoughts, that we can't direct our feelings may sound unbelievable to most of us, but as soon as our thoughts and emotions are seen as a series of appearances on a screen, it is obvious that we are just *being lived*. Even the ideas of choice, regret or guilt are images passing by. We are all actors playing the role we are designed to play. Although the judging mind doesn't like it, we can see that everything is happening as it is supposed to be happening. Everything is as it must be![18] What is, is. Just like a shadow isn't responsible for its movements, we are not responsible for what comes up in our minds. And if we can't choose our thoughts maybe we can't choose our actions either. When that's clear, all sense of guilt or pride melts away. This doesn't mean that we now become serial killers or terrorists. We continue to live as before but all those habits of criticizing ourselves and others can fall away. Imagine how many internal dialogues would disappear. If there is no free choice, it is also clear that every moment of our life up until now has been absolutely appropriate. Not one step could have been taken differently. Everything you apparently did couldn't have been any different! We are just actors in a movie, acting and reacting according to our conditionings. Our programmes just respond to the circumstances. When we see that we can't manage our thoughts, there is a sense of freedom that arises, because now we see that everything is just happening as it is happening.

Still, people will argue that they feel as if they really decide themselves, and it is true that the sense of free choice looks real and convincing. That is exactly how the daydream is designed.[19] But the question whether we believe in free will or programming is still based on the concept of time and the concept of being a person. What if we see through the illusion of time? What if we see through the illusion of being a separate identity? All these philosophical discussions are irrelevant when it is understood that both theories are built on quicksand, as they still belong to a personalized point of view. As soon as it is clear that the person (who is supposed to have free will or not) is purely conceptual, all these discussions are like arguing whether dragons are male or female. Such discussions become ridiculous as soon as someone points out that dragons don't exist anyway. Once it is clear that the person itself is a concept, an idea, all the rest is clear immediately. Then, all questions about free choice or predestination evaporate.

A DAYDREAM

Some people say that life is like a movie, like a daydream. It means that all objects and all beings (including ourselves) in everyday life are merely illusory phenomena. They are appearances with no real substance, similar to what we perceive in a dream during sleep.[20] While we are dreaming (lucid dreams apart), we don't realize we are lying in our bed and we believe that the perceptions in the dream are real. We – as the main character in the dream – pretend to be the subject (the main character) living in a real world with other characters and objects around. While we are dreaming, we don't realize that all the characters and objects in our dream are fabrications of our mind. It is only when we wake up the next morning that the dream is labelled as having been unreal – only an appearance in the dreaming mind.

It is obvious that we could tell a similar story about the waking state, the so-called daydream. Every object, every experience is a thought form. Perceptions appear to our waking consciousness in a similar manner as in the dreaming mind: they are phenomena in our brain, they are images in our consciousness. Here again, we play out a role with the 'me' as the actor and the apparent world as the scene. But how real is the scene? How real is the main character? How real is the border between the character and the world? How real are the thoughts and emotions in the daydream?

Let's go back to the dream when we are asleep at night. Suppose we feel thirsty in that dream, the illusory drinking of illusory water can quench our illusory thirst, but all of this only seems real as long as we don't realize that the dream itself is illusory. And we could draw a similar scenario for the so-called real world. Does the world exist by itself? Are we a person living in a solid body? Or is it indeed like a daydream? Is our body ever seen without the aid of the senses and the mind? Is the universe ever seen without the aid of the senses and the mind? Is there a world outside our knowledge? Or is it just a creation of our brain? We all know that the world is filtered through our senses and understanding. If our senses had been different, the world would have appeared quite different. Is the so-called environment around us really a separate object existing outside of us? Or is it just a series of images?

What is the use of saying that everyday life is an illusion, a daydream? Does that really change anything at all? Does that insight bring us closer to our true nature? And what about waking up from the daydream? Is it possible to see that everyday life is indeed like a construct of the mind? Awakening sometimes seems to appear as a sense of the world being a construct of the mind, and the personality being an *instrument* of Awareness. Some people report that they feel as if things are being done through them. The habit of identifying with the doer may fall away. In the Buddha's words, 'Events happen, deeds are done, but there is no individual doer thereof.' Others seem to come into 'this' by the sense of the *watcher*.

Most of us can understand the metaphor of watching our life as if we are watching a movie. While we are reading these words, we know that there is something watching us reading these words. We can check that out right away: there is a neutral witnessing that allows us to see what we see. It is not a second head watching over our shoulders, it is our clear Awareness which is witnessing what happens.[21] Still others report an opening of the heart, they feel a sense of unconditional love, of divine stillness, and associate liberation with (their) sense of love and peace. Others recognize all this but can't put a name to it and accept the names given by a spiritual leader. They might call it divine love, or the higher energy of their soul. They may describe this pure Beingness as the love of Krishna, as pure Buddhahood or as the love of Jesus. Or they follow the tradition of their spiritual organization and talk for example about the *soul* that is supposed to have a higher goal, or a divine energy that gives them inspiration, or a divine entity that guides them to salvation. All these stories are in some subtle way still about 'me'. No matter how divine the description, or how peaceful and loving the transcendental experience was, there is still a process of personal claiming going on.

Although there are no stages or steps to take on a 'path', one could say that both the sense of being 'an instrument of awareness' as well as being 'a witness of what is' are intermediary steps between the habit of identifying with the adult personality on the one hand and naked (unidentified) Beingness on the other hand.[22] When the sense of identification with 'me' also disappears, there is only a clear witnessing of what is. Then there is no instrument of awareness, only clear awareness. Then there is no witness, only neutral witnessing. When the daydream is an illusion, then the daydreamer is an illusion as well.

What sometimes happens is that after a transcendental experience, the witness is still personalized in some subtle way, for example by identifying with the instrument we believe is giving rise to our deeds, or by locating it somewhere behind the back of one's head, or in the heart or soul, or by associating awareness with a sense of watching the world from a distance, from a higher level. Maybe we imagine that now we are a seer, sitting in a chair watching our movie on a TV set. There is still some identification with a watcher sitting at a distance, a neutral witness behind a wall of glass. We should remember that when the outside world is an illusion, an image, our personality is also an illusion. If the others are phantoms then we are a phantom, too. We can't pretend that 'we' are real and that the rest of creation is just 'maya', just an illusion. Whether we believe we are an instrument of Unicity or whether we think we are a witness of our movie, as long as we limit ourselves to this instrument or this witness, there is still a subtle process of identification going on.

SELF-ENQUIRY

Self-enquiry is often suggested as a way to realize our true nature. But who is going to make that enquiry? Who asks the question, 'What am I?'. Where is the Self? And is this Self separate from us? How can we look for what we *are*? How can we ever *not be* what we are? Is-ness has never been far away but one could say that we simply overlooked it. Many have been struggling to change their conditioned patterns without realizing that what they're looking for is that which is closer than their usual sense of self. A glimpse of that which is free of such conditioned patterns may be an invitation to have a second look. To reconsider our usual sense of self, we have developed increased interest in personal growth and contemporary spirituality, but many seekers have been disappointed in their psychological and religious adventures since these usually fail to fulfil their promise. In fact, after several decades of spiritual practice, many seekers recognize that all these belief systems and spiritual practices are food for their own minds and as such (apparent) obstacles to awakening. Spiritual organizations tend to perpetuate the belief that true awakening is not for you and me, and projecting it onto spiritual heroes is a popular game among seekers. If Beingness is personalized in this way, it will additionally be projected into the future as a (personal) reward to be obtained after a lot of effort or good luck. As a result, Beingness is not presented as that which is fully available right now.

Many seekers today are no longer interested in something that takes several decades of meditation; they are thirsty for a true fulfilment which is accessible and available to them as they are – not as they should be. Such approaches are sometimes described as nondual teachings, because they point to that which cannot be cut in two. These teachings don't divide

Oneness into good and evil, they don't project Awakening into a future state. Such teachings – teachings isn't the right description of course – clearly postulate that what we essentially are is already immediately available. They also emphasize that this Liberation isn't a personal trophy, and is within everyone's reach. There are only a few teachers who don't compromise in this matter.[23]

Just as our hands are designed to grasp things, our minds are trained to get hold of concepts, but awakening is completely beyond getting anything. This book is about the discovery that we don't have to look for anything spiritual any more because everything we are looking at *is It*. Oneness is obviously reflected everywhere. There is simply no way to escape from Is-ness. So there is no need to change our life style, open our heart, still the mind or even overcome our conditioning. Any teaching that suggests the seeker should be different from how he or she is at the present moment confirms our sense of separation, and is only feeding the mind which wants to change things. It keeps the seeker on the spiritual path. Such a teaching serves the ego's need to perpetuate its own spiritual search. All these personalized teachings can attract the mind for a while because they give people hope and temporary satisfaction.[24]

Our minds will try again and again to split Oneness into parts. The mind can't help doing so because that is the way it is designed. Our minds will even try to turn the recognition of Beingness into a process, cut Unicity into pieces and then suggest that the goal is to bring the pieces together again. The seeker then asks what we can do to get it, to understand it, to feel it. Our mind will even create a guru who will show us the way up the mountain, but once Beingness is recognized as Oneness, it is clear that there is nothing to be recommended. Any teaching that recommends us to do something, any book that gives us hope, starts from a basic misunderstanding. Any suggestions on how to be more available to Beingness are in fact subtle ways to postpone the immediate direct recognition of Beingness. Seeing Is-ness can't be planned; the anticipation alone is the most effective way *not* to recognize It.

When we see that all the boundaries we create are only games of the mind, the clarity that is the source of all this becomes self-evident. Usually, there is less resistance, less opposition to the flow of life. One could say that we become more fluent, more transparent, but who would be there to report or even notice that? There is only this, and 'this' is life happening, simply everyday life. We don't wake up in a new and magical world. The daydream just goes on. Ordinary life just goes on, and when we say ordinary we don't mean uninteresting or dull. When the judging mind loses its power, when it's seen that presence is all there is, ordinary moments can become sublime and filled with timeless presence.

The mind wants to divide the world and everyone in it into good and evil, into body, mind and soul, into past, present and future. All these divisions keep the game going. It's essential to make the movie look real. That can go on for a while because we can produce fascinating theories and beautiful stories with all that.[25]

But basically, we can't compartmentalize Unicity. We are Unicity appearing as me and others, each with an individual story. Although it looks very real – as real as a good movie looks while we watch it – it is still the play of the One pretending to be many. It is clear that the character holds onto his own story, and everything which is personal is considered most important. We all tend to hold onto our personal drama, as well as that of other people. We also want our life to have meaning and purpose, and we usually hate it when someone says that life is a movie, that all our personal struggling is only a metaphor. Although there is a wisdom in us that recognizes that our life is a parable, we usually resist the idea and prefer to continue to take the daydream very seriously.

The ego wants a target to aim at, a goal to work for, a special path to walk, and will never accept that there is nowhere to go to find Beingness, that there is no path to follow to become enlightened. The mind will try to tell us that it will take us to enlightenment through a process, by working it out. Liberation has nothing to do with hope and effort but with being childlike and being in wonder at what is.[26] Still, the professional seeker prefers a path, a goal. One may even come up with a technique to become more childlike, or try to be more flexible, try to accept everything as it is. One of the most popular goals in the spiritual path is trying to live in the 'here and now', and the problem appears when this is interpreted as a new task, when 'living in the here and now' is presented as a new personal goal. Where is this person who is supposed to be 'in the here and now'? How can we *not* be here? How can we *not* be in the now? Even when we think about our holiday in France last summer, our thoughts are still here and now. Here and now often suggests the existence of a 'there and then' which refers to a process in space and time. All of these concepts are toys of the mind – the Light doesn't care or even know about these.

Another popular task is trying to get rid of our thoughts. Thoughts are sometimes presented as an obstacle to awakening, as a disease of the human mind. The ego is also presented as a problem, or at least a false concept to be transcended, but who is going to do that? Trying to get rid of or transcend the ego is like taking hold of ourselves around the knees in an attempt to lift our bodies off the floor: the more we pull, the harder it gets. We may imagine that with practice we will finally succeed: we work out to get stronger muscles or we try to lose weight in order to be able to lift ourselves up one day. As long as we believe we can lift ourselves up, we will continue our spiritual search, although all our attempts to attain the final goal are doomed to fail. Even when we can actually jump in the air, it will only be for a second. The only escape here is to let go the idea of being a person who needs to be lifted up. In other words, as long as we believe we are a seeker who needs a spiritual peak experience, as long as we believe we have to develop our 'higher powers' first, we are doomed to believe that we must become better or more spiritual.

THERE IS NOWHERE TO GO

When the penny drops, it is rather like a switching off, as if the clock has stopped ticking: there is no longer a sense of a personal past or future – although such images can still appear (in the timeless Light) for practical reasons. We give less importance to our personal past and future. This means that speaking about 'before' and 'after' the penny drops is incorrect, and so is the idea that 'you' are going to drop your penny.

It all looks like suicide for the spiritual seeker. One could say that it is nothing awakening to everything.[27] It is no-one realizing nothingness, and this nothingness is witnessing life happening. It has nothing to do with detachment from the ego or non-identification with the doer, because there is no-one to do the detaching or stop the identification. The wonder of Presence is that there is nothing we need to do to get anything of It. Beingness *is*.

We have been so well taught and conditioned by centuries of belief systems that we are not in touch with that which is infinite. We have invented philosophies, religions and spiritual techniques to help us in this direction and there have been prophets and gurus to point to the way back home. When we realize that the infinite is everywhere, we may understand that all these stories can be windows to a broader vision but we may also see that we don't need all this. There is nothing to find out which is not already here right now. There is only the awareness of what is, and that is enough. That awareness is exactly what we are. It is not somewhere else. Christ said, 'The Kingdom of Heaven is within you', and that is exactly where some teachers say we should look, within our very being. That doesn't mean somewhere inside our body, heart or soul, because this Beingness can't be localized. Once we recognize that the Kingdom is without boundaries, we realize that 'within us' means everywhere because the Light is everywhere. We have learned to identify with our person but that is no more than a concept in our minds. We are beings that have forgotten that we *are* being.

There is a story of a prince in seventeenth-century Siam (now Thailand) which explains how our true nature has only seemed to be lost. The king of Siam lived in Ayuthaya, the capital of Siam at the time, with his wife and seven daughters. He desperately wanted a son. When his wife got pregnant again, she gave birth to a boy. There was a big party in the palace to celebrate. Six months later, the royal family took their boat to spend the holidays in their summer palace, on the island of Koh Samui. When they crossed the Gulf of Siam, they were surprised by an awful storm. The waves were so high that water came into the ship. The water was rising so quickly that they all went upstairs to the roof of the boat in order to escape from drowning. The king was holding his son in his arms. Two of his servants had already drowned. When they were standing on the roof and saw how dramatically the water was rising, they realized that there was no escape. The only thing the king could think of was saving his son. So, the king put his son – a baby of six months – in an old wooden box. Eveyone drowned, but the box floated away on the tide and the prince was the only survivor of this drama.

The baby was found later by a young woman on the coast. She took the baby with her and raised the young boy as if he was her own son. Two days later, she moved to a village in the north of the country (now Chiang Mai), where she worked in the local market. At the age of fourteen, the boy also worked in that same market to help the fish dealers. When he was eighteen, he left her and moved to Ayuthaya to work there as a fish dealer.

One day, a Buddhist monk passed by. This monk had been a close friend of the royal family. He used to visit the king and his family on a regular basis, and sometimes lived in the palace as a guest for several weeks. While this monk looked into the eyes of this young man, something amazing happened. He recognized him as being the king's son who survived the disaster twenty years ago. So the monk went to the fisherman and told him that he must be the prince who survived the boat drama, saying he recognized him by his eyes and his facial expression. The young fisherman didn't believe the monk, claiming that he was just a fisherman. 'Look at my clothes,' he said. 'Do I look like a prince?' But the monk wanted to be sure and contacted the relatives of the royal family. His uncles also seemed to recognize him, and they found a black birthmark on his neck, exactly as his father had! When he was told about the typical birthmark, he allowed himself to be open to the idea of actually being a member of the royal family. When it was finally confirmed by his uncles, the young man gave up his resistance. He also remembered that his mother had told him she was in fact not his real mother but that she found him on the beach. Although he couldn't believe it, although he remembered selling fish on the market of Ayuthaya even that same morning, he had to accept now that he really was the prince, and so he agreed to be taken to the palace. A few weeks later, there was a big ceremony in Ayuthaya. He was crowned as the new king, and learned to perform his royal duties.

In this story, the recognition of royalty stands for the discovery of the Kingdom of Heaven. Someone else pointed out that the young man was already royalty. *He just didn't recognize his real identity.* It was the Buddhist monk who recognized him, and his uncles had to convince him of his royal identity. Although he resisted the idea in the beginning, at some point he finally accepted his true identity.

The question is, what exactly was different after the recognition of his royalty from when he was at the market selling fish? Even before he was recognized as a prince, he was actually the prince too, although nobody knew. The point is that he didn't know that he was royalty originally. This is precisely how it is with our spiritual search for the Kingdom of Heaven: we are the Light from the very beginning, but we identify with a limited personality. We *are* princes but we believe we are fishermen. We are already Beingness but we think we are separate individuals. We go through our lives thinking and acting like spiritual seekers, we walk around looking for paradise, without realizing that the Kingdom of Heaven is already here. We are royal from the very beginning, without noticing it. And deep inside we know this, but we can't believe it. We are looking for our palace, while we are actually Home all the time.

One day, about a year later, our prince – now the king of Siam – woke up with a strange feeling. He was tired of performing his royal duties. He started to miss the simplicity of his previous life. He became homesick for the life he had when he was selling fish in the market of Ayuthaya. He changed his clothes, walked down to the fish market, and without telling anyone about his plan, he took up his old position, and started to sell fish. And things were just as they had been before – he was selling fish again, nobody knew he was actually the king of Siam, and in a way he enjoyed returning to his old life for a day.

The second part of this story illustrates that after awakening, we can't lose our true nature. Even if we seem to lose our understanding, even then we are still royal. Even when we have doubts, even when we don't behave like a king, even if we return to our old conditioning, that same Beingness is still there. So, even when we (apparently) return to normal everyday life, we are still royal. Finally we understand that how we behave or what we look like is not important. We don't have to behave like a saint. It isn't necessary to change our clothes or our diet. We don't have to sense a perfume of peace, we don't need to feel the Kundalini rising up our spine, we don't need to clear our chakras first, we don't have to neutralize our bad karma, we don't have to feel unconditional love all the time in order to belong to the club of enlightened masters. After awakening it is clear that *everyone is royal* and it is also clear that this was the case before that realization. There is no before or after. Oneness is borderless. Nobody can be excluded. That is quite evident since nobody can live outside the Light, no matter how this apparent person is behaving. We can forget about what all these so-called sacred texts are prescribing. There are no rules, there are no prerequisites. Even when we live an ordinary life, we are still in the middle of the Kingdom of Heaven. We don't have to wait until we die to enter heaven. There simply is no escape from Beingness, whether we live in the royal palace or sell fish in the marketplace. We are all royalty in disguise.

NOBODY IS EXCLUDED

When the penny drops, everybody is enlightened – and nobody (as a person) is enlightened. *Everybody* is enlightened because we can't point to anyone who is not expressing Is-ness and at the same time *nobody* is enlightened because a person – a phantom – can never own Oneness. The actor can never claim the Light. When we see that there is only Light, when we see that Light is all there is, it is obvious that we are all the very same One. We are all Beingness appearing as separate individuals.

If Beingness is all there is, why do we look for something more? Maybe we want some higher state,[28] maybe deep down we want peace of mind, or maybe we just want to get rid of our personal problems. Maybe we are proud to be a famous seer, maybe we want to be proud of ourselves because we are working towards a better world. Maybe we look for harmony and abundance. We may be proud that we have meditated twice a day for twenty years, maybe we want to be like our spiritual hero. Is Beingness about wanting something for ourselves? Is this book about being successful on a spiritual level? Is Oneness about getting in a higher state of consciousness? Is this Beingness about excluding what we don't like?

The Unicity pointed at in this book embraces *everything*. This Light doesn't judge or compare. Nothing or nobody can be excluded from This. Just as they are *is It*. Just as we are *is It*. Even the border between them and us is seen as conceptual. We are no longer burdened by this weight of past concepts. The three belief systems we talked about before lose their power, and usually life seems to run smoother without the weight of all these rules and codes. It becomes clear that there can't be high without low. It becomes obvious that there can't be a battery with only a positive pole. As a result, the need to fight evil loses its importance. The urge to change others drops away. The sense of having to be different from how we are melts away. Each moment is fresh, each moment is met without an agenda. When ordinary life is met without a personal agenda, 'our' responses may not be coloured by labelling and expectation. When there is no personal baggage, the response can be spontaneous and unpredictable.[29] We may find ourselves sitting in silence, and at the same time there isn't anybody sitting here. That person appears to be the origin of our world, but where is the centre of our frame of reference? This role we play looks like the central manifestation of presence, but that idea is also an image passing by. All we (who?) can 'do' is realize our own nonexistence. It sounds like an impossibility or paradox but it comes down to nothingness discovering what it really is like.[30]

In fact, we could say that on a spiritual level there is a complete disintegration of any sense of me. Seeking is spontaneously dropped. What falls away is the belief in the one that looks for something higher, and there is no person who can do anything about this. Seeing that leaves us with nowhere to go: it is the end of spiritual business because there is no more 'me' to identify with, who can look for profit by practising meditation or by behaving in a particular way.

WHO IS WALKING THAT PATH?

Still, the need to 'do' something is very strong. We want to work towards a better world, we feel we have to fight injustice, and we believe we have to work on ourselves. One of the tools the ego uses to polish its spiritual image is meditation. Although meditation can seem to be a door to Oneness, it is usually regarded by the seeker as a technique to attain a higher goal. There is nothing wrong with meditation, it is *the belief in the meditator* that causes the spiritual search to go on. This identification with a spiritual seeker usually prevents meditation revealing that there is nobody there. If that belief in the doer falls away, there is just nothingness. Such a 'meditation' is spiritual suicide. When it is revealed that there is nobody sitting silently, there a different perspective. All methods require a *doer*. All spiritual volition is a manifestation of the me-concept. Who is praying? Who is meditating? Who is prescribing Self-enquiry? Who is doing Vipassana? Who adores the Lord Shiva? Who is doing Bhakti? Who is devotional to whom? Who is doing Zazen? Who wants to be liberated? As long as Liberation is sought under the compulsion of the seeker's mind, how could it possibly be realized? On the other hand, as soon as the concept of being a seeker disappears, it is clear that Liberation is never absent. When this mistaken identity with the seeker is seen through, it's obvious that there is no spiritual path from here to there, from now to later. Any path can only lead us away from home, and we can never get away from home. Home is everywhere, so believing in a path is also 'it'. In other words: dualism is also 'it'. Home is timeless and pathless and as a result apparently seeking and not finding 'it' is also an expression of Oneness. Believing that there is a spiritual path is also a pure reflection of Unicity. Finally there is no escape. All is one.

The common belief that enlightenment means we are in a fixed state of bliss, peace and goodness usually comes out of the stories we have read in books on Eastern mysticism. There, enlightenment is often presented as a state someone has attained once and forever. These people are then described as sages or avatars, and obviously they are considered to be on a higher spiritual level than you and me. Some of them are presented as being superhuman, with special powers and divine qualities.[31] That is not the Liberation this book is pointing at. Beingness has nothing to do with a state. At some point we understand that what we truly are is stateless. It is a non-localized presence. This timeless welcoming is our true nature. There may be a subtle sense of just being present without identifying with a seeker. What is absent is any sense whatsoever that what is witnessed should be other than it is.

WHO WANTS TO BE ENLIGHTENED?

When the seeker itself is seen as conceptual, all the rules of spiritual organizations become obsolete. As a result, we may lose our moral code in spiritual matters. Although we still have to play the game of living according to the rules of society, we can lose our compulsory need to judge and criticize. We can also lose our sense of having a past and a future, of having a personal story. Such a loss may feel uncomfortable in the beginning, but once we realize that what has been lost is just a construction in the mind, we see that it was never owned in the first place. It seems to be a matter of dying, but what dies is only a concept. To some, however, the familiarity of the challenges of the personal story are more attractive than the recognition of empty Beingness. In other words: they prefer the perspective of having a life story. They prefer to continue daydreaming, they prefer the role they play. And in this role, the personal emotions, memories and hopes are given a lot of attention: it all comes down to the personal drama. The daydream is all about the personal adventures of our 'me'. It seems to be more fascinating for the mind than the neutrality of pure Awareness. They prefer to continue to identify with the role they play (and that is OK) and take it all seriously. This allows them to judge and criticize others, to take the holy books seriously, to believe in karma and reincarnation, to worship Krishna, to hope for a reward, to believe in heaven and hell, to work for a better world, and so on.

Most seekers seem to like this personal drama. They prefer to try to be good, to have a sense of responsibility, to work on a more spiritual life. Trying to work towards a higher level of consciousness – whether on a personal or global level – is like trying to run a battery with only a positive pole. It is like trying to find Utopia. We can imagine we are working on a landscape with higher mountains, but this means that the valleys will look deeper. Although it is very attractive for the mind to be a good citizen, to work on a better future, it is not possible to run a battery with only a positive pole.

Beingness can be described as neutral as it has no position on matters of right and wrong other than to allow both to exist (in our minds). Seeing that both black and white are parts of the daydream can lead to a witnessing which is transparent and non-judgmental. That doesn't mean we become lazy or indifferent. The role we play seems to go on. This witnessing doesn't exclude being egocentric or helping others – both are equivalent expressions of Is-ness and seem to depend on the conditioning of our (apparent) personality and the circumstances of the (apparent) environment. The recognition of this Beingness allows both acceptance and nonacceptance, both peace and war, both truth and lies, but advocates neither. Good and evil are just two sides of a coin and only exist in the individual's mind. Beingness itself just is … what It is. As pointed out again and again, Beingness is reflected everywhere. So it doesn't come from somewhere or go anywhere. It has neither a specific location or point of view. It has no specific characteristics. Beingness is both in the high and the low. We will never know what Beingness really is. One minute we think we see It and the next minute we believe we have lost It. But It can't be seen or lost because Beingness is equally in the seeing as in the ignoring. Beingness is always on both sides of a coin. In fact it is in the whole coin too, and it is even in the absence of the coin.

The very wish for awakening is a continual denial of our nature as already being awakened. The Light doesn't need to be lightened up! When awakening apparently happens, it is seen that there never was (and is) anyone who was *not* awakened. As a result, it is obvious that one can never *become* awakened.

As a result, 'before' and 'after' awakening don't apply here. There is no process from unawakened into awakened. The idea of awakening is only of interest for those who believe they are a separate character. They hope that they – as a person of course – will become awakened one day. The better spiritual technique, the better partner, the better guru: all of that can seem to be able to make our daydream more appealing, but it will not give us Beingness. We *are* Beingness.

It may be clear that there is no way to describe the indescribable, and as a result all descriptions of enlightenment in this book are doomed to fail. Nobody has ever had the capacities to understand or describe enlightenment, simply because the tools of the mind are limited. And the enlightenment we are referring to here is That which is without limits. So we can't pretend to have recognized Oneness, all we could say is that It is impersonal Beingness *seeing Itself.* Beingness playing the game of separation by mirroring Itself through more than six billion body-minds. Still we all feel as if we are living as separate persons on this planet. We all feel like a black dot surrounded by other black dots,[32] and we seem to be surrounded by billions of 'other' people who also feel the same: they also seem to feel separate.[33] How do we reconcile this feeling of separateness with the recognition of Oneness, as described by all these mystics and seers throughout human history?

No borders

As newborns, there is no separation. There is only Unicity – although we don't realize it as such. In other words: as newborns we have no limits: we are sand (without realizing it) and don't limit ourselves to one particular body (one particular sandcastle). While growing up, we've (apparently) lost this

Unicity as we started to believe in 'me' and the others, good and bad, high and low, past and future, cause and effect. The adult vision corresponds with our sense of being limited to our body and mind. As adults we usually feel separate: we feel like a sandcastle that is obviously different from the other sandcastles. Although 'our' sandcastle is made of the same sand as the other sandcastles, each castle seems to be separate from the others. Awakening could be described as the recognition of the openness of the newborn. There is a rediscovery of the impersonal quality of our true nature. This impersonal 'vision' is the open attention of undivided Beingness. It corresponds with the limitless nature of the sand on the beach. Since both the beach and our sandcastle are made of grains of sand, our true essence is recognized as 'being sand'. This sand is the ground of our Is-ness, the light of our life, the essence of what we are made of,[34] and it is clear that this sand is the same for the (apparent) others. This is what we all share, this is what we all are, and as such the difference between 'me' and the others becomes purely conceptual. Then it is clear that 'you' (as Beingness) are everyone. All borders are gone.

Still, many spiritual seekers who are looking for their true nature continue to focus on the growth of their own sandcastle. They put all their interest in their individual path and are still hoping to win the golden medal one day. They believe they have to prepare themselves so that eventually they will attain spiritual enlightenment. They want it for themselves, not for all of us, but true spirituality is not a match they can win. There is no path up the mountain. The problem with the idea 'of reaching a higher state in the future' is that it is based on personal thinking, on judgmental thinking and on time-related thinking. All three are practical in terms of organizing society, but are completely counterproductive when it comes to Liberation. Awakening reflects the knowing that there are no borders, that everything is-as-it-is, and that no amount of seeking or understanding can ever change that. It is not about changing the quality of the images on the screen, it is more a matter of recognizing the Light in these images — no matter what kind of images are appearing on the screen.

CAN WE FIND WHAT WE ARE?

How hard can it be to rediscover our true nature, if our true nature is what we really are? How can we *not be* what we are? And what about our sense of being a person? Where is this seeker dwelling? When we close our eyes for a minute and take the time to find where our personality lives, we only find a concept. We can witness the functions of our body, but when we try to find an ego inside our body, we can't find it. We have to admit that we will never be able to find such a person inside because we just know it as an image in our mind. The same goes for our so-called soul. We can talk about the soul and invent as many theories and stories as we like, but nobody has ever seen a soul — except as an image in their own minds. And what about Beingness? Can we find where that One is living? Our true Essence is not to be found because it is everywhere and as such, is invisible to the seeking mind. Beingness does not live somewhere inside our brain, it isn't just another image appearing in our mind. It is That in which all images appear.

Usually we live with the assumption of a 'me' that resides in our body, animates our thoughts and looks for spiritual freedom. When that assumption falls away, we are stripped of our most cherished idea of 'me' and we melt into what is. When the 'me' falls away, there is only *this*, and 'this' is what is appearing in 'our' attention — nothing more, nothing less. Then there is an intimacy with everyday life we never imagined before, without anyone there to feel intimate. The word intimacy is misleading because all borders are conceptual anyway.[35] Without any sense of control, motive or choice, things are just happening. The mind–body dichotomy falls away, the belief in karma and reincarnation drops away, the separation between good and bad disappears, the me–others dichotomy collapses, and all that is left is a clear witnessing (by nobody) of what is.

WHO DIES?

When there is identification with the person who is supposed to be living in our body, we all have to live with that most inescapable of certainties: the common-sense fact that we are lined up in death row awaiting execution. There is no question of whether we die, but only a question of when we will die. However inevitable death may look, the crucial consideration is whether death really is the end. Can we accept the fact that the light will just be turned off? If we are made of perishable stuff, there is no other solution: once we are dead, the game is over. Once the heart stops beating, the brain will run out of oxygen and quite soon after that, the movie is over. Still we feel that this can't be true. Our body may be made of perishable stuff, but what about our soul?

Because our personality finds it hard to accept the fact of disappearing, we invent the existence of a soul, and this leads to fascinating stories about an afterlife or reincarnation. Especially when we are not clear about what we really are, we are likely to cover our fear or uncertainty by such games of the mind. Of course, nobody *knows* how it feels to die or what exactly happens when our appearance falls back into Beingness. But on the other hand, it may be possible that the Beingness which is available right now is exactly the same as the Beingness that awaits us when we die.[36] When we die, the film runs out but the Light is still on. Beingness doesn't stop when the film stops, because Beingness has no limits in time and space. It is immortal, it is endless. When it is clear that the 'me' is purely conceptual, then both birth and death must be conceptual too. It is like water recognizing wetness. When the concept of 'me' melts away, death is like an ice cube melting in a glass of water.

With the sandcastles metaphor in mind, we could say that each of us is a living and walking sandcastle, (apparently) separate from the other sandcastles because it has a different shape. From a personal point of view, we do indeed seem to have an individual shape. Each of us has a unique genetic code, a unique body with an unique manifestation in this (apparent) world, and our senses (especially the combination of vision and touch) confirm each day that we seem to be separate, that each of us is a person living in his or her private body. That's the basic element of the opera. The whole game seems real as long as we (who?) identify with body and mind. But what if we identify with our true nature? What if the water in the ice cube sees that it is water? What if the light in the actors 'sees' that basically the actors *are* the Light? As soon as we understand that we are sand rather than a sandcastle, it is clear that all separation is in our minds and as such conceptual. As a result, our identification with this body is conceptual too. What we essentially are – Beingness – has no limits and can't die.

In the movie of 'our' life, the living creature seems to disappear when it dies. When the character dies, he won't be acting any more. As soon as the sandcastle is destroyed, it disappears into the rest of the beach, and its unique shape is gone. From dust to dust, from sand to sand. The game is over. But at the same time, its true essence – being sand – has survived physical death. What happens is that the body-mind machine dissolves into the pool of Beingness, just like a wave that disappears in the ocean. Realizing this, it is interesting to note that it doesn't really matter what form the sandcastle has, because it is the same sand anyway. From that perspective, physical death is in a way complete liberation. We return to what we are, which is Beingness. We are back Home. Well, nobody is actually going anywhere, it is Light seeing Light. We must keep in mind that nobody ever comes Home. It is an impersonal Liberation.

THERE IS ONLY ONE

If this book wants to address Unicity, there can't be two or more of them. That may sound quite obvious but the mind is designed to make Unicity *appear* as separation, the Singular *appear* as plurality. However, this mental process is unidirectional. It doesn't work the other way round: we can't bring the pieces back into oneness. The mind is like a pair of scissors that can (apparently) cut a piece of paper in two, but these same scissors aren't able to join the two pieces into one. The scissors can't 'cut' two pieces of paper into one. In other words: the mind can't turn dualism back into Oneness, it's impossible. [37]

The mind will never understand Awareness. The seeker will never get it. We can think about Unicity and even try and describe it, but these words are never Unicity itself. Our mind always turns everything into a concept, so it will also try to turn Awakening into a concept; but the concept of Awakening has nothing to do with Awakening itself.

All ideas of 'becoming' are rooted in the same ignorance: the idea that there is somebody who has to go somewhere, and that somewhere is usually more special and holy than 'what is' right now. Liberation is seeing from nothingness, from neutrality if you like. It is the opposite of specialness. It is absolutely ordinary and magnificent at the same time. But some spiritual seekers want to imitate their heroes, they want to win the spiritual lottery, they want to make a deal, they want the ultimate climax, they want a life without any problems, and they all want it for themselves. This is spiritual egocentrism. It is amazing to notice that what the spiritual seeker desperately longs for more than anything else is actually totally simple and immediately present. It is the One that is the very substance of ourselves and the world. It is the very essence that all our concepts and beliefs are made of.

WHERE IS GOD?

Before religions became organized, they were originally based on direct insight in the nondualistic nature of Is-ness. In the course of time most of them more or less degenerated into conceptual knowledge and rigid belief systems, pointing the aspirants in precisely the opposite direction to that in which the final truth can be found.[38] This is done by splitting Oneness into two (dualism) by referring to the separation between good and evil, between past and future, between samsara and nirvana, between phenomenon and noumenon, between God and his creation. Each culture and religion has its own sense of what is right and wrong. The purpose of some religious leaders is not to help the seekers discover the truth for themselves, but to impose their own story on their followers. They pretend that something is wrong with us and that they will bring us to salvation.

With the metaphor of the ocean and the waves in mind, we know that we are all waves appearing in the same ocean. We seem separate but we are all one, and we are all made of water. But the spiritual leaders tell us that we are so dry, and they say we have to follow them in order to become wet again. Once it is clear that water never lost its wetness, all their religious codes become ridiculous. How can water become more wet?

What can the wave do to become wet? Follow another wave?

Some religious leaders believe that their view is the one and only truth and usually suggest that the spiritual techniques of other religions are misleading, wrong and even dangerous. Religious leaders sometimes present other belief systems as unworthy, untrue or even hostile. They all pretend to start from the same Creator but by giving a different name to that God they create a very fertile breeding ground for religious conflicts. The history of the last two thousand years shows that such mis-understandings can escalate into conflicts again and again. The leaders of some religions seem to want their religion to grow, they want their particular system to expand. They believe that others are living in darkness because they are not following the rules of their religious system. They consider the influence of their religion as more important than the core message of the origin of their own religion, which says that we are all the very same One.

As an actor in 'our' movie, we usually believe that there is a producer behind our story, someone who created all the stories, who created this universe and laws of nature. But the Light is both actor as well as director. Still, theories of cause-and-effect are very popular in this matter. They are attractive for the mind of the seeker who loves to believe in a personal story. They underline the importance of the person who takes credit for what he has achieved. We see ourselves as creators. Religious organizations extrapolate this theory onto a wider scale. They suggest that a higher energy or divine being has created the universe. As long as spiritual seekers don't recognize naked Beingness as their true nature, they will accept or believe such stories. They may project a creator onto the universe and call it God (or whatever name they are told within their cultural or religious background). Many people believe that something superhuman created this cosmos, that some higher intelligence organizes all this energy and information that builds up the wonder of the cosmos as we know it. If we are an engineer and see how complicated it is to build a car, we can easily extrapolate this idea of an engineer onto the cosmic creation. When people see the complexity of life in the rainforests and the oceans, when they realize the intelligence of the human body, when they think about the capacities of the human brain, many seekers tend to project a higher being that is standing behind all this; a divine being who created it all.

The believer in God usually separates himself or herself from Beingness by projecting this Beingness onto some higher intelligence. It suggests that the seeker is separated from this higher being. This higher intelligence watches us like a father and may even reward us or punish us according to our behaviour. Such a belief only confirms our conviction of being separate from Beingness and 'not good enough'. The term God usually suggests perfection: God is only good and loving while our human behaviour is often labelled as sinful. Looking for an explanation for the bad things in life, a devil is made up to explain where all the evil in the world is coming from. Each religion creates its own system of standards for divine and evil, but nobody has the universal standards to say what is wrong or what is right. Ultimately, neither good nor evil has any substantial existence, except in the minds of the believers. The terms good and bad can be useful tools to organize everyday life in society but when it comes to Beingness, such a division creates a rather artificial situation. Beingness is beyond all dualities. Translating this into religious terms, we would say that God (as 'Beingness' or 'Light') is neither good nor bad but neutral, but that's not very attractive to the mind.

Those who believe in a separate God, and a world created by that same caring God, may finally see that the separation between God on the one hand and the creation on the other is completely artificial. It is another example of dualism, and so is the division of the world into heaven and hell. When spiritual leaders are asked how an omnipotent God allows evil to exist, they get into trouble. Is this God not supposed to take care of his creation? If God is trying to prevent evil, but is not successful in doing so, what is his power then? Isn't he supposed to be almighty? When he has the power, but doesn't want to prevent evil from appearing, does it mean he deliberately created suffering? If he is trying to teach men a lesson, why would he do that? What is all this suffering for? If God created the *entire* universe, doesn't it mean that he also created the shadow parts of it, both the good guys and the bad guys?

If we accept for a moment that indeed God created the universe, aren't we supposed to respect the Creator for what he did? How dare we criticize his creation then? Isn't the devil also a part of God's creation? And how can some religious leaders have the pretension to suggest that there is something wrong with the world? How respectful is that towards the Creator? We must be careful to use the word 'God' as an entity separate from its creation. Where exactly is the border between God and his creation? The word 'Beingness' or 'Light' is more neutral than the word God and doesn't suggest any separation between the One and the other. That is why in this book we suggest that there is no separation between creator and creation. It is all Oneness, and if there is a God, this God must equal this Oneness.

When we realize that we are not separate from God, that doesn't mean that we *as a person* are God – that would be blasphemy. The person we think we are has nothing to do with this, we are referring here to what we really are – which is Beingness. And that Beingness equals God. When we understand that we are not apart from Beingness, that the Light is equally in the projector as it is on the screen as it is in each character of every movie, we stop making all these distinctions. We don't go on looking for an explanation or consolation and we automatically forget about the projection of a creator of the universe. Creator and creation are projected everywhere without exception. The cosmos doesn't need our ideas about a creator in order to unfold as it is (apparently) unfolding. When our minds are creating a creator, it is because we believe in time and space, in cause and effect. A lot of seekers seem to like the idea of such a higher intelligence (whatever form this belief may take), because they start from a personal view and project it onto the Infinite. One of the reasons they do so is that they take comfort in the concept of such a higher being. Such a story explains some unanswered questions (or at least, it seems to explain them!) and it gives them temporary consolation. They usually don't realize that they make up these stories themselves in order to keep the personal game going.

Once the Unicity of all creation is clearly seen, we no longer need to project Unicity onto a higher being. One glimpse of Oneness may be enough to blow away all our old beliefs and concepts. Then the need for an image of something superhuman disappears immediately. The belief in an ultimate creator is simply the ego's attempt to give a name to the unnameable Beingness. It is like a movie actor who is trying to give a (holy) name to the white light coming from the film projector that he senses is creating and directing his unfolding film. Once it is recognized that Light is all there is, all our old belief systems lose their importance.

When we see that what we *are* is clear Awareness in which everything arises, we rediscover a very subtle form of childlike wonderment; a sense of being that doesn't depend on our personal circumstances, that doesn't depend on our feelings or thoughts. Our conditioning may still label sadness as bad and happiness as good but now it's clear that the ups and downs in life are inherent to human everyday life, and are unavoidable as such. Sadness can equally be witnessed as happiness: both appear on the same screen. The screen doesn't care what appears on it. With no attachment or involvement, there is no attempt (by the Light) to suppress what is witnessed. Our personality may still feel involved, but that sense of being involved is again an image appearing on the Screen. One could say that the ups and downs are allowed to play their game. When it is seen that there is no up without a down, life can flow more naturally. There is just a neutral transparency watching us and the world as one timeless image.

This recognition of Oneness is the core element of all the nondual traditions. We can describe this Oneness as timeless, because it is out of time. We can describe it as impersonal because it goes beyond the personal life story. We can call it 'a-causal' because it has no cause. We can describe it as unmoving because it is not going anywhere. So there is no need to run after it because our running after it is also it. There is no point in turning our back to it, because turning our back is also it. There is no need to wait for it: our waiting for it is also it. Whatever 'we' do or 'the others' do, it is all an expression of Beingness. Once we put in perspective the framework of thousands of years of spiritual traditions, we may rediscover Beingness in simple everyday life. We don't need the holy scriptures, the candles and the incense. We can forget about what the priests have been telling us for so many centuries. There has been a labelling of people as sinners, as failures. We have been told by religious leaders that there is something wrong with us, but is that really the case? And on what terms can anyone say that? It all depends on what framework one uses. Once that game is seen through, the issue of judging and sinning is over.

Still, a lot of spiritual teachers seem to operate from a

specific framework. They can't help it acting as they do. People can't help it because that's the way their mind is designed. Those teachers who are still talking from a 'me' position attract those seekers who want to attain something for their 'me'. Such teachers usually suggest that we can reach the same spiritual level they pretend to have by following their dogmas, worshipping their gods, praying their prayers, meditating regularly, reading their books, changing our diet according to their rules, being very serious about the teaching, maybe changing our clothes, taking the spiritual name they give us, being very moral, and so on. The final goal is sometimes presented as the reward after taking the five steps to the top.

As said before: the Awakening referred to in this book is totally beyond any path or ripening process because it is clear that it is completely beyond the reach of the person we think we are. As a result, it has nothing to do with becoming more holy, less neurotic or more peaceful. It all comes down to unmasking the belief systems that we have been taught while growing up. When we see that Awakening involves realizing what we are *not*, all the stories about enlightenment lose their power. Then we dispel the myth that the 'awakened ones' must have had good luck or that they only became enlightened through various rigorous spiritual practices. The Awakening we refer to in this book is not a personal achievement, and has nothing to do with a person claiming or spreading 'the truth' to his or her devotees. This text is not about spiritual heroes, it is not about miracles or religious experiences. It is about Beingness, it is about what we *all* are.

A lot of mystical literature has stimulated spiritual seekers to expect ecstatic peak experiences, because they are full of stories of special people who claim to have attained so-called higher states. Maybe some of them really are in a state of higher consciousness, but does it really matter? Isn't the division between high and low levels of consciousness an example of dualism? Isn't the border between the sage and the average seeker another form of separation? Is Beingness interested in the hierarchies of the conceptual world? Is Oneness concerned about the games played in our minds? Does the Light make any difference between samsara and nirvana? Is this quest about examining other people's states? And if all is One, where are the so-called others? What is the point of comparing? Where are the boundaries? Who is separated from whom?[39]

WHO IS FOLLOWING WHO?

Stories about religious leaders and enlightened masters are of course very popular. Because the seekers desperately want such a state of bliss and perfection when they hear or read about them, a series of expectations is created. At the same time, while seeing that they are far from perfect themselves, those seekers may feel quite frustrated because they see their problems and longings and suppose that these enlightened teachers don't have any problems anymore. When we feel that something is lacking in life, we go and look for a solution. We may consult a book or a teaching, or someone who apparently has solved all his problems, or an organization which pretends to know all about this subject. If we want to play the role of a student, we create a teacher who will guide us to where we want to be guided. That is a position where we are vulnerable and liable to believe without questioning. We do whatever we are told to do because we have implicit faith in our leader. We presume that we don't know and that the spiritual leader who pretends to know will solve our problems, answer our questions and maybe guide us to salvation.

We may say that teachers are a matter of taste: for every devotee there will be the perfect match. Some seekers look for

an enlightened master they can devote their life to. They believe
their master is important and has spiritual powers. In some
cases, the specialness of their master reflects their own need to
be special, too. Some look for the familiar paraphernalia of
satsang – a teacher dressed all in white, eye-gazing, transcendental happenings, portraits of gurus, flowers, emotional releases,
burning incense. It's all very attractive for the heart and mind.
The seeker wants so much for a teacher to offer solutions to his
problems, and there seem to be many teachers who pretend to
have the answers. Some of them will work on our emotional
problems, others will focus on our deepest fears, and suggest
they can work it out for us. Still other spiritual leaders will use
our hope to become enlightened to make us do what they
want us to do. Both seeker and teacher then play the game in
which the belief is held that the teaching is perfect and that
the teacher will lead the devotees to perfection. Any form of
criticism is out of the question, and the fact that the seekers
believe they are not enlightened but the teacher is, only
confirms the distance between them. It is again the game of
separation – although they won't call it that and rather say it is
'the way to complete salvation' or 'a sharing of divine love' or
'the one and only supreme path'.

The division of the One into high and low is very attractive:
high energies and low energies, spiritual people and ordinary
people, holy books and evil books, good leaders and bad
leaders. Such hierarchy is also quite common in spiritual groups
around a master. In other words, the nondualism of the nature
of Liberation is avoided in order to continue the game of
separation. As long as the guru is special and the devotees are
ordinary, the devotees can continue to play their own game of
denial of their true nature. The majority of the seekers prefer
to stay seekers: they prefer to be devotees at the feet of their
master rather than recognizing their true nature. All these

situations clearly show that both teacher and devotees are still in a subtle game of separation[40] between high and low levels of spirituality, the match between the good guys and the bad guys, and so on. A lot of it originates from the need to make things better, the belief in a hierarchy, the belief in a process, playing the game of going on a path, looking for a spiritual goal. A lot of such spiritual teachings are based on three things: ignorance, egocentrism and business. Ignorance because Oneness is split in two or more: It is split into good versus bad, past versus future, while the nondualistic nature of Beingness receives no attention. Egocentrism because it is all about personal attainment: it is all about 'me' getting somewhere. And business because it is about a teacher and seekers making a deal where the seekers are stimulated to follow the rules of the club. Like faithful dogs, the devotees are willing to do anything for their master because they hope for a spiritual reward.

Some teachers don't need us to put them up on a pedestal, they don't want their listeners to fall into idolatry, they don't care about appearing imperfect or having shortcomings. They stimulate us to focus on Beingness and not on their personality. They invite us to see the message and not pay attention to the messenger. They force us back to the utter simplicity of what is, without any spiritual specialness. They don't tell us about their own master all the time, they don't pretend to have had the highest enlightenment experience possible, they don't pretend to have transcended their ego, they don't promise to bring us salvation, they don't give us any hope for a better future. All they do is unmask all these games, and tell us that we can only be as we actually are, not how a spiritual leader or a holy text suggests we should be. They will not encourage us to compare our 'spiritual' story to theirs or to other people's stories of their spiritual experiences. They tell us that awakening has nothing to do with imagining that there are bigger awakenings to be had. They explain to us that people can't be divided into enlightened and unenlightened. They say that when the search ends, everything is divine. All the colours of life are allowed to appear in the Light. The dark colours and the bright colours are equally 'expressing it' and there is no hierarchy. In other words: even the bad guys are divine! When the spiritual game is unmasked, everybody is the Guru. Everybody. Even the liars and murderers are appearing in the Light – no more and no less than the saints and the gurus. Even the shadow sides of life are holy. Both sensations of anger as well as love are expressions of Oneness. Everything is Beingness, everyone is enlightened. It is the end of all prescriptive measures, the end of trying to be a good ghost, the end of trying to polish the mirror, the end of trying to join the club of the masters.

When a teacher claims to be 'an embodiment of truth', when he suggests that you should – just like him – sense the perfume of peace all the time, when he says you should only have positive thoughts, when he suggests that his teaching is only for the ripe souls, when his ashram is called 'the House of God' or 'the Abode of the Absolute' or when he claims that 'his heart is awakened to the whole ocean of reality', all these statements are very attractive for our seeking heart and mind.[41] Especially when they give us hope that we can also become like them. It becomes even more misleading when we actually *feel* this openness and peacefulness when we are in his (or her) presence. We may get addicted to the sensations that go with such encounters, and we may conclude that we have to feel that way all the time.

We should realize that Beingness isn't about me and others. Beingness is not a matter of experiencing bliss and peace at the feet of the master. Some will indeed open our heart, clear our mind, and let us *sense* what this clear presence is supposed to feel like. All of that can be very sensational and blissful, but some of these experiences only make it more confusing and difficult. Although such experiences can be windows to impersonal openness, they can easily stimulate the game of separation between devotee and teacher, between peak experiences and ordinary life. In that way these special experiences can be very misleading.[42]

If the teacher claims to own and express pure Beingness, the devotee is likely to project It onto that particular person. As said before, it is very attractive to the mind, especially when the guru is intelligent, beautiful and charismatic, but such situations reflect a subtle process of personalization of the whole enlightenment issue. This infinite awareness can't be locked up in a guru. There is no way of localizing Oneness. That also means that It can't be limited to a religious text, a holy mountain in Israel or in South India, a Buddhist temple in San Francisco, a spiritual place in Tibet or a Shiva temple in Texas because it is equally reflected *everywhere*. Some teachers say their ashram provides a supportive environment for those who wish to realize the infinite within themselves. Each time there is a subtle suggestion that Oneness is more available in a certain person or a specific place, the limitless nature of Beingness is avoided in order to play the game of separation. We can forget about the holy river, the incense, the holy mountain, the altar and the candles, the holy textbook, the Buddha statues, the Shiva lingams, the sacred mantras and all the religious rituals. Attractive as all of these seem to be because they pretend to point us to Oneness, they rather point to high and low, they divide between spiritual and not spiritual. They confirm our interest in hierarchies, they feed the mind's need for division and dualism.

No hierarchies

Beingness is not exclusive to gurus, avatars and the bodhisattvas, it is for you and me and everyone else. Nobody is excluded from It (because we are It). It is so ordinary, so obvious, so natural. Most of us seem to fail to just recognize It, and that is also part of the opera. Taking the movie seriously is part of the role we play in that movie. And even when It is (apparently) recognized, a lot of seekers fail to believe that It can be as simple and obvious as that. They prefer the drama. As a result, we don't realize that *this is It*. Everybody is living in this vastness, we all have an awakened nature but we are not paying attention to It. Some teachers say that when we are paying more attention to this ease of being – through a simple switch of perception – we are allowing our attention to rest in this infinite emptiness.[43] In this emptiness there is at the same time a wholeness: everything is an expression of the infinite, completely as it is. This infinite Space is not some kind of spiritual Utopia or paradise, it is the most common place on earth: indeed, we can recognize this Infinity both in the sunset over the ocean and in pain, failure and ugliness. Once Beingness is recognized as impersonal, we can see it in the guru as well as in our neighbour next door. Once Oneness is seen for what it is, it can be seen in both the holy scriptures as well as in the newspaper. Any discernment between holy and profane is artificial; the difference between samsara and nirvana is even ridiculous now.

What we call Space is like an empty container: it is all around us but has no specific location itself. It has no form or shape, it cannot be cut in two and at the same time it is the background in which everything appears. Any object has a location to a reference point, and is contained in this same Space, but Space itself has no location. This Space is like a screen that remains untouched by what happens on it. A novel may describe the wetness of a mountain river, but the paper itself will not get wet. Similarly, Beingness remains pure and unaffected by its content, and at the same time it is not at a distance from what appears on it. The separation between the Screen and what appears on the screen is also conceptual. The separation between Space and what appears in that Space is conceptual, too.

But if there is only one Oneness, why are we splitting It in two again and again? Why split It into a holy and an evil part? Why are we creating all these spiritual paths? Why are we projecting the infinite in a spiritual hero? Why do people believe that they will get rid of their sins when they wash themselves in the Ganges river? Why do we want to have mystical experiences? What is so fascinating about the story of Krishna and Arjuna in the Bhagavad Gita? How can an author suggest to his readers that they can find God through sex? Why does a so-called teacher of Advaita suggest that his ashram in Texas provides a supportive environment for those who wish to realize the infinite within themselves? Why are we so interested in transcendental events? Is the actuality of everyday life not enough? Is there something wrong with life as it is? Without our mind's interpretation, the world as it appears in day-to-day life *is* already whole and undivided. That is what is sometimes understood after a transcendental event, but the danger is that the mind – after the event – comes up again with the old programmes and belief systems. The mind will whisper, 'You had it for a moment, but now you've lost it again. You must work on yourself in order to get worthy again. You have to be more serious about enlightenment. Look how blissful the real sages are. You are not there yet.' When there is no clarity about our true nature, we may easily fool ourselves and get into the seeking process again. Any attempt to try to be other than we are is only diverting us. Any game of comparing is a reflection of our lack of understanding. It is such a relief to see that Liberation has nothing to do with self-improvement, nothing to do with the fulfilment of our personal wish list, and it may be a relief for some of us to see that we are not a failure that needs to be fixed. Liberation is not personal, and ironically our seeking obscures the obvious fact that Beingness is already available for one hundred percent.

Do you want more?

As soon as it is clear that Beingness is reflected everywhere, there is no point in trying to bring peace and bliss into our lives, or to try and work towards a better world. Trying to express Beingness in a spiritual way is just a game of the mind. To try and change life which is already changing all the time is an unnecessary struggle. Life is always changing (apparently), the only non-transitory factor is Beingness itself. It is impossible to make life more holy. It is a mind game to say, 'I have seen Oneness, and since that magic moment it is ripening and stabilizing more and more'. When we believe that first we have to see It and then we have to live It, we are back in the horse race. Beingness cannot change, cannot evolve, it is only the conceptual world of the mind which seems to change all the time. The personality is fascinated by the ripening process because it is all about 'me'. So, the seeker hopes for a better future but both the person and the time frame are illusory, and so is any sense of ripening.

The belief in a seeker originates from the belief in a personality and the belief in a process. Practical as both may be in the conceptual world, such beliefs do not bring us closer to Beingness. It is like a wall of glass between the 'experiencer' and the experience. Once the illusory aspect of this wall is seen through, the wall of glass is broken. When this happens, it may feel blissful. It can even appear in the mind as a major transcendental event. But we don't have to destroy that wall of glass over and over again. The sound of breaking glass may be sensational, but the process of destruction can't go on forever, unless we are building up this wall of glass again and again. And we can apparently continue to do so until it is realized that there never was any wall of glass between subject and object.

Only those who feel bound can perceive a sensation of freedom. If we want to have that feeling of breaking free again, we will have to lock ourselves up again first. But what's the point? If the penny dropped, why pick it up again? In order to drop it again? As soon as the prison is seen as illusory, there is no more need to go back into prison in order to experience the escape from that same prison once again. Feeling free or feeling locked up: both are expressions of the infinite. When that is seen, plain ordinary life can be enough; nothing is lacking and nothing can be excluded. Everybody is invited to see that the prison they think they live in is made of a web of (self-made) concepts and beliefs.

As said before, the attachment of the seeker to struggle is common. Most of us have grown up with the conditioning that we have to 'do' something with our lives. We are supposed to make our lives work.[44] That may look appropriate in the field of education but when it comes to Beingness, it is rather counterproductive. Learning how to use a saw can turn us into a good carpenter, learning how to control a ball can turn us into a good tennis player, knowing about the rules of Hinduism can turn us into a good Hindu, learning how to control our breath can turn us into a good yogi, but nothing can bring us closer to Unicity. Although it all sounds attractive, trying to be a good boy or a nice girl will not bring us closer to Beingness.

It is amazing to notice how teachers who claim to talk or

write about nondualism are still working towards a better world, still worshipping Shiva, or suggesting that they have actually attained the highest state after a long and difficult journey. It is all very attractive to the phantom, of course. It gives the seeker something to hope for. Giving the phantom something to do gives it a sense of being real and confirms its sense of separation. Overcoming the difficulties on the spiritual path gives life a purpose. Trying to imitate our spiritual hero gives life a meaning, a spiritual goal to aim for, but this struggle also leads to a continual disappointment. In most cases, the goal is not reached, and if we believe that it is attained, we fear we will lose it again. Or we doubt that it is already the real liberation and we believe it has to ripen: we have the silver medal and are still waiting for the gold one. Having a spiritual goal keeps the seeker running on the wheel of struggle, hope and disillusion.

All these expectations and time-related processes only deny that life is living itself for (and through) us. When it is realized that the ego is not the doer, it is clear that we don't lead life but life is led through us. A ghost can't drive a car, although it will claim to be the driver. A phantom can't make any decisions, although it will claim to be responsible. Or other phantoms will tell you that you are responsible. It's all part of the game of life. We can't make life happen, life happens through us.[45]

We don't have to do anything to let this river of life flow as it flows, and trying to manipulate the stream only prevents us from letting life be smooth and easy. We put ourselves at the centre of a cause-and-effect game, but these laws of cause and effect and the belief in past and future are concepts of the mind. The gift of life is to let it all happen, not try to engineer it into something more spiritual. Finally, it is not about seeking and it is not about stopping seeking. If we decide to stop the seeking because we heard that enlightenment is the end of seeking, we still have an agenda: we stop seeking because we want to reach something.[46] We want to reach non-doership. We want to accept life as it is because that is what some teachers suggest. We want to be one with nothingness, we want to feel Beingness and we are willing to imitate our spiritual heroes for that. It is just a trick of the mind imitating what the teachers are saying. It is a game of the ego that wants to join the club of enlightened masters.

When we try to get rid of our conditioning, we may see that this is an endless game. All we can reach is the new conditioning so that we don't recognize our old conditioning any more. Claiming, 'I am not the body, I am consciousness' is another concept, another image of the mind. Even trying to be without any conditioning is another goal, another conditioning. Maybe living a conditioned life is inherent to human existence. Freedom is not to be found in getting rid of our conditioning, but to see the illusory aspect of the whole game. Does it really matter if the ghost seems to be conditioned? The apparent personality may seem to resist certain things, but Beingness can't resist anything. When we accept all our conditioning and belief systems for what they are, there is less need to control or programme life. Even the need for transcendental experiences falls away. Who would have these experiences? And what for? As soon as the prison is seen as illusory, there is no longer any need to break out. The only one in the prison is a ghost. In other words, the prison is empty. As soon as the 'me' is seen as illusory, who needs to break out? And where does the ghost need to go then?

THE END OF SEEKING

When the Light is seen (by nobody), it is like watching the blank screen (or the light of the projector) in the movie theatre.

It is not you or me seeing it, it is Light seeing Light. Then it's said that pure Beingness shines in its full glory because it is not overshadowed by the pictures appearing on the white screen. Although this is an impersonal and timeless happening, it can be very inspiring. All the apparent characters in these movies are manifestations of the infinite appearing as a divine play in one big show, and the magic is that this Presence and all these manifestations are even not separate. They *are* One. Everybody moves in That, is That and comes from That. Even when there is an apparent moving in and out of this vastness, it is clear now that even then we are still 'in the middle of It', and never separated from It. The feelings and sensations we believe we have don't matter any more. Whether we feel identified with a depression or whether we feel open and blissful, it all appears in and as the same Is-ness. And Is-ness is expressing itself in so many ways. Identifying with the image of our personality is only one of the many expressions of It. This Oneness can't be limited by anyone, can't be broken by any idea and can't be attained through any experience. It is just that which perceives *everything*, without there being any boundary between It and what appears in It. The mind can never say, 'Now, I've got It. Now I am enlightened, finally.' Saying that presupposes some entity that was separate from It and now has got It. This is impossible. We can never have It or for that matter we can never lose It. How could we lose That which is borderless and timeless? What we really are has no desire for enlightenment. What we really are has no fear of ignorance. Beingness doesn't care about misleading teachings. Dualistic teachings are equally an expression of Is-ness as non-dualistic teachings. So, there is nobody to be criticized.[47] What we really are, is free from all that comparing or criticizing, and encompasses all that as well. Beingness isn't interested in our spiritual experiences, isn't interested in our hierarchies. Oneness doesn't consider worshipping Shiva as more important than driving a taxi through London. Beingness doesn't consider praying to God as holier than drinking a glass of wine. The moment we cling onto any concept of enlightenment, we are playing games again.

Having had a transcendental experience, reading about this subject, talking with teachers of the nondualistic schools, all of that can indeed remove ignorance, just as light can dispel darkness. This can happen in a split second: when a light is switched on in a dark room, the darkness is gone immediately, no matter how long the darkness (the ignorance) may have existed. But even when the white screen is not apparent any more because we are again hypnotized by the images appearing on it, the Light is still on. Even when darkness apparently appears again, Oneness is still here. This Light is never switched off. Even at night, the sun is still shining. Even when the king of Siam goes back to the marketplace to sell fish, he is still the king.

Once the game of the mind has been seen through, there is no way back. If the Light is not apparent on the surface of the screen, then our minds can conclude that It must somehow be covered over. We wonder what it is that constitutes these coverings, and we wonder if we can learn to remove them in order that the Light may be seen again. That is one of the mechanisms to get back in the spiritual horse race. How could the infinite ever be covered over if it is infinite, if it is all-encompassing? The coverings are also part of that same infinite! Maybe there is nothing whatsoever to remove. Maybe we don't have to turn our attention to the Light instead of the images appearing in it, maybe we just have to see that both the light parts and the shaded parts are equally expressions of the same Light.

When what is pointed at in this text is clear, limits and differences are still witnessed as before, but it is clear that these borders are conceptual and only have apparent value in the organization of everyday life in society. In other words: there is no longer a central figure in the daydream. The idea of bodily sensations being localized is very strong because that is how the senses and the mind are designed. The sense of being in a body can still appear 'after' the penny drops. We believe there is a central figure living inside of us: that is how we are programmed, but at the same time it is obvious that the only central and permanent element is the Light, not the actor we think we are.[48] Instead of saying, 'I am hungry', we should say, 'there is hunger arising'. Instead of saying, 'I am brushing my teeth', we should say, 'there is a reflection in the mirror who is apparently brushing teeth'. That sounds a bit strange, so we continue to play the game of separation with the so-called others. Separation includes love and war, joy and pain, democracy and terrorism, health and disease, birth and death. That is how colourful life can be, and as in a good movie it all appears to be very real: the pain, the joy, the sense of separation. It's all part of the show.

Unmasking the game of separation doesn't mean one escapes from ordinary life. The apparent opera goes on looking real even after the penny drops. Language still makes it sound as if there is a person living inside our body, but even while we play the role, it is clear that everything is as it is. That goes for the other characters too: they can't help being as they are, they can't help doing what they do. If they are so and so, they are so and so. Allowing everybody and everything to be as they are can take away the judgmentalism and the seriousness out of our lives. Our story, the world's story, the religious dogmas; it really doesn't matter.

When the penny drops, all that happens is that the seeker vanishes. When it is clear that the separate you is a ghost, the seriousness about the personal story drops away. The spiritual stuff especially has no more meaning. There is a certain lightness about life, but there are no promises, and no characteristics describing how one should be after awakening – there can be no demands or obligations if the personality has nothing to do with this. Awakening has no special merit because there is no person who is awakened. There are absolutely no reference points to awakening at all. Beingness is not a state, it is timeless and so has always been – it has never appeared and then gone away. It is 'flat' seeing in the sense that it comes from the sourceless Source, from the neutrality of the Light. No here, no there, there is just what is. Some refer to It by talking about the 'way of the heart' or 'the salvation of the soul' but talking about the heart or the soul is again a subtle way of the mind to try to localize It while It is everywhere. This Beingness cannot be localized or associated with a personal emotion or attribute. Is-ness is not some subtle energy that is floating around and that we can catch by using a technique.

It is often suggested that when things are seen without an internal dialogue, everything and everybody can be seen as they are. Then pain is said to be seen with the same neutrality as pleasure, although the senses are still conditioned to prefer pleasure to pain. Some teachers say that there will be less importance given to satisfaction versus frustration. The personal preferences are allowed to appear, but the mental battle is said to be over, and even when there is some mental resistance to what is appearing, that is also an image appearing and disappearing. Trying not to be judgmental, trying to be peaceful and loving, being frustrated that we don't get it, trying to turn the world into a better place, all of these are just images appearing in Awareness. And as pointed out before, Awareness doesn't care. To simply let desires and ideas flow without interference is what can happen when personal investment disappears. The central personality who is supposed to deal with all this is seen as conceptual, and then all the rest just flows. That can be the end of the self-reflective mind, but not necessarily so: we should remember that an internal dialogue can also be part of the flow.

So, what is left now? Just Beingness, being in being, without any boundaries. That is all there is. Then, there is nothing to hold onto because one person is not considered as higher than another. All these insights are of course a threat to the person's central position. The mind can't get this. Beingness is completely beyond the ego's capacity to understand. The recognition of Beingness as unattainable for the mind is a direct threat for the seeker. As said before, in order to postpone his own unmasking, the seeker may come up with a new plan. One of the plans is to get 'it' in the future. So, in order to maintain his central position, a lot of beliefs and expectations are created again and again. Even after reading a book that unmasks all the spiritual games, the seeker will creatively come up with some personal story again. But Beingness has no dependence on what our minds think about it. Beingness has no time reference and no personal reference. When that is clear, the house of cards topples down. The personal story is unmasked. Where is the person who is supposed to have preferences, where is the one who is holding on? Still, the (conceptual) show goes on: there seems to be a life story played out by a person with memories, emotions, preferences and expectations. That is exactly how the daydream is engineered. Our senses, our conditionings, all of that is allowed to continue – there is just a greater picture that is seen (by no-one).

LIFE GOES ON

Without the 'me' there is no search, no spiritual goal, no looking for something sacred or divine, no meditation techniques, no more questions and answers. The paradox of the spiritual search is that what is sought is Beingness. We say we want to become more open to Beingness, but openness suggests that we can close ourselves to Beingness. That suggests there is a barrier between 'me' and Beingness, but there is no barrier! We *are* Beingness, there is no escape from it and there is no way to open ourselves to it. Personal processes – no matter how spiritual or important they may look – can't get us nearer or more open to Beingness. Once Beingness is recognized as It is, all the holy scriptures lose their impact. They can still be pointers to Oneness but they are not Oneness itself. In fact, nothing is *not* sacred any more. Exactly as we are right now is a perfect expression of Beingness.

Is-ness is not all glossy, blissful and attractive. If that is what we expect, we will be disappointed. Beingness has no quality of goodness or holiness about it, it is completely neutral. Recognizing It will not turn us into better people because Liberation cannot be related to goodness or badness. It is beyond all that and also embraces all of it.

Liberation is not a matter of becoming cold and indifferent, but exactly the opposite: all borders and hierarchies are gone. All the images of the personal story still continue to appear in Awareness, but they are seen for what they are: seemingly temporary snapshots. They are not what we *are* – even when they appear to be very personal. The whole appearance of what we call our person acting in the world will apparently go on and on, the rules of society will still be there, but now it is seen as one great play, a divine play with only one player appearing as more than six billion players. Some describe it as a divine play, as an expression of unconditional love, as a mirroring of the One being. Although nothing can be recommended, it may come down to letting there be feelings, letting there be thoughts, letting there be lust, letting there be thirst, letting there be conceptual thinking, letting there be laziness. What is, is. And to 'do' so, there is no magic formula, no magic key, no special trick.

Three:

Dialogues on the Nature of Oneness

In the following interviews, you will notice how difficult it is to talk about Beingness. Still, there is a repeated pointing to the immediacy of this presence in almost each conversation. When two or three are together to share in this kind of communication, an openness and spaciousness can arise which is very familiar and yet ungraspable. It is about the recognition of the ground of Is-ness in all there is.

In these conversations, I didn't try to focus too much on the personal aspects of the stories but rather to That which is available for all of us. And That is what we all *are*. However, since It is completely beyond the framework of our mind, all these dialogues will fail in describing It. The drawback of personal stories about enlightenment is that they point to that which seems to be different between you and me, and that is precisely what this book is trying to avoid. Additionally, the reader may try to identify with the specific succession of events presented by the teacher and conclude, 'It has not happened that way for me, so I must not be awake yet. I still have a long way to go.' Additionally, all these stories have a beginning in time, and as a result are not the infinite itself, but glimpses or experiences of that which is beyond the mind.

It is true that some teachers seem to be clear about nondualism. Although there can't be any rules or guarantees, it is often suggested that being in the presence of these people can be a catalyst in the recognition that this Oneness is what we already are. It is interesting to notice that being with those who 'woke up' from the daydream seems to stimulate in some way our own recognition of what we already are. At some point, it looks like a transmission of the flame. That can be quite misleading for the reader because it may sound like there is a new goal, which is to go and look for the real masters; to go and sit close to that rare teacher who doesn't compromise about nondualism. That's another trick of the mind to reinforce your sense of separation. The Light doesn't want or need anything from you because the Light only sees Light. What you do or believe can't change that.[49]

Still, there are many reports from seekers who say they woke up from the daydream while being with their guru. They say that before the penny dropped, the importance they gave to their belief systems was maintained by being with other people who were also holding to the same belief systems. They believe that the daydream of their imagined life story continued to look real until they met their master. Being with their guru apparently woke them up. All these stories are very attractive to the mind, because it suggests that meeting someone who woke up can have a similar effect on yourself. Again, this is about spiritual materialism.

When hearing about these stories, people are willing to give up their 'normal' life in order to have a spiritual life – for example at the feet of a guru in an ashram in India. From a personal point of view, there seems to be a transmission of the flame, but Oneness itself can't be transmitted from one person to another.

Although you know that everyday life is the real guru, meeting teachers who communicate this can be both confusing and inspiring. Some people are scared to discover that their personality is but a phantom, others are relieved to see that there is nowhere to go. I've met several spiritual teachers, although not all of them were very clear about the nature of Oneness. Some teachers were obviously leading people up the garden path, while in most cases they were even not aware of it themselves. As soon as I noticed some form of hierarchy or seriousness in the spiritual field, I knew I was dealing with a teacher with an agenda. That doesn't mean it was not interesting to have a conversation with them, or that they are wrong and I am right. Some teachers claim to talk about nondualism, but when you take a closer look at what they're saying, you notice a lot of divisions and discrimination between this and that, higher and lower, positive and negative, right and wrong.[50] Others had a clarity and straightforwardness I still appreciate, while others were projecting their own denial onto me, or were still operating from their own moral code. Others became dear friends.

In the conversations that follow, you may resonate with some parts of the dialogues as they reflect an issue you're interested in at that moment. Other parts may evoke resistance, and some dialogues may awaken a 'knowing' that has been within you since your early childhood. Each conversation may have something that resonates with you. You may also notice that despite the diversity of their cultural and religious backgrounds, these people finally agree that there is only one truth, and that each of us is already that Oneness, despite the differences in expression. You may be fascinated by the fresh uniqueness and by the limitations in the ways this same Awareness is being expressed. You may just get irritated by the fact that the same things are being said over and over again. Maybe the words in this book cut through your confusion about enlightenment, perhaps they don't.

Sometimes you may encounter certain parts in the conversations where there is a subtle tendency to personalize the enlightenment issue, or that the reader is told he or she has to be a certain way. This is almost unavoidable since any conversation starts from words, and words are always conceptual by nature. All these words are mere pointers to Oneness, never an attempt to describe Oneness itself. So, don't focus too much on the words themselves but on That which they are trying to point at. As Zen Buddhists say, 'The finger pointing at the moon is not the moon'. You may notice that in some conversations Oneness is subtly suggested to be a personal trophy that can be attained, but it is clear that there is no person to lay claim to This. Although these interviews seem to suggest that there is a person called Jan who met other persons in his quest, and through meeting these others discovered what he was looking for, it isn't like that at all. This story of seeking is another series of images appearing in the same Awareness. It doesn't mean anything: it is just the story of a ghost meeting other ghosts. I know it looks like a real story while you read the interviews, but the conversations have nothing to do with me or anyone else. It is only about Beingness recognizing Itself.

At some point in my apparent life story, I believed I was still going in and out of this Oneness. That belief was a reflection of my lack of understanding at the time. Before I met Tony Parsons, I still believed there was somewhere to go, something higher still to get. Subtly I was hoping something special would happen to me. Until the penny dropped and it became clear that Unicity is all there is and that there never was any Jan to get it or not get it. After awakening – if one can use such words because there is no Jan who woke up – the apparent story goes on but there is no longer any seriousness about the spiritual path. The phantom called Jan seems to go on playing its role but it is clear that nothing is going anywhere or has some purpose or some higher meaning. It is the end of the spiritual journey, the end of the longing for the holy grail.

When it is clear that there is nowhere to go because there is no seeker in the first place, all spiritual paths become obsolete. All religious codes lose their meaning. Most seekers hate that idea, but some understand that practising a technique or method is a reflection of the misunderstanding about the nature of Liberation, since it presumes that there is a journey towards That which is already the case, and that there is a practitioner to practise a spiritual technique. Being attracted to a technique shows that you feel as if something is still missing and that you need a path to go towards it. It is futile to practise presence because it can't be practised. It is also futile to try not to practise it. It is equally futile to try and do nothing because trying to do nothing is just another technique. So I can't suggest anything, not even trying to be here now, being ordinary or being available for presence. I'm not interested in making you better or more ready for It, because the 'you' you think you are is a phantom and the 'you' you really are is already That.

The phantom is a master in the game of separation and appearing real. It will use all its means to look like a real person, not like a role played in a movie. The character wants to survive by delving into the personal story and by asking why, when or how. It will use all its means to focus on the personal aspect again and again, but the Light is not interested in your character. Presence is not involved because it doesn't have any investment in 'your' story at all. Everything arises out of that source of Light, and that Source is not a concept or a higher being which is separate from the rest.

Don't think you will ever work it out: you will never understand Is-ness. It's a mystery. It is the energy of presence, which is so immediate that you can't notice it. It is even directer than direct because you're not separate from it. It is more than always and everywhere, it is all there is. There is only one image that appears to be a series of images that build up a story. Your story, my story, the story of the world, the evolution of the human race, they are all part of the opera. There is no time process, so there is no cultural or spiritual evolution of mankind. But there is still very strongly an *appearance* of human evolution. The mind creates a time frame because the character can't operate in its movie without taking the concepts of past and future seriously, and that goes for both the apparent individual as well as for the apparent world.

When the penny drops, there is absolutely no more sense of how you should be or behave in order to become worthy for enlightenment. There is no need to change the character (the 'me' you think you are) because you are already a divine expression of Oneness. Nothing and nobody needs to change. A good character or a bad character, does it matter? Whether the penny drops or not, who cares? Nothing needs to change. It is the end of trying to make a deal with life. You (who?) are not separate any more, not alone any more, because all there is is all-oneness. When there is no 'you' there are obviously no 'others' and there is only 'what is'. As said before, when the sense of separation loses its importance, you don't walk around in permanent bliss. It's just the falling away of the belief that you have to be a certain way. So it is obvious that I don't want to suggest or pretend that I am permanently in Oneness – that would be a contradiction in terms. As I said before, Jan has nothing to do with This, and I am not claiming that I can try and talk you into this Oneness. I don't see any need to change you or anyone else. Why should I when I have understood that everybody is This. When your penny drops, that is OK; if you prefer to continue to believe in the daydream, that is equally OK.

Some apparent seekers who read or hear about all this seem to lose themselves. They give up the idea that they can get somewhere – not because someone told them that there is nothing to do to get enlightened, but simply because the game of the separate identity is unmasked. Then they get absorbed into a stream where spiritual games are given up. It looks as if they have given up and let themselves float with the current of life happening. At the same time it is clear that there is no-one floating. There is nobody coming home to their true nature. All there is is what happens. Maybe you would prefer me to make it more complicated, more attractive to the mind, but It is so simple, so natural. There is just what is.

The invitation is always there

JK: Many seekers think that they have to live or behave in a certain way in order to become enlightened one day. One of the characteristics of your teaching is that this is not necessary at all.

TP: Trying to change your way of life is another barrier. Liberation is simply sitting in what is, without any idea of becoming anyone or changing anything. It is just what is. Isn't that amazing? And somewhere we know this, somewhere inside we recognize this: this is It! Liberation is not something to be found somewhere, or something to be obtained in some imagined future.

JK: In your talks and in your book *The Open Secret*, you don't give the listeners any tools. What you seem to do is blow away their belief systems, take away all their hopes. And you don't give them any homework.

TP: That is the most powerful way of avoiding Liberation: by looking for it, by working on it.

JK: The first time I saw you in London, you said, 'This is It!' with such conviction, that it really did strike me. Afterwards, I suddenly realized that I didn't have to go anywhere, that I didn't have to go through a process of purification in order to find Liberation.

But still many seekers feel that they are not there, that they haven't yet found Liberation. So, there is a problem: you say it is already there and at the same time the listeners sitting with you in that room feel that they haven't seen it yet.

TP: The problem with people sitting there and listening to me saying that, is that their mind is thinking that this so-called 'It' should be different to *what is* at the present moment. They want something to happen. They expect some sort of sign, and they want something different from what is actually happening. People are not prepared to really fall in love and let go into 'just This'. It is too ordinary, they want something spectacular to happen, they want the fireworks.

JK: I think Eastern mystical literature has stimulated the so-called spiritual seekers to expect all these ecstatic peak experiences, because they are full of stories of special people who have attained so-called higher states. Because the seekers desperately want that state of bliss and perfection, they create a series of expectations. And at the same time, while seeing that they are far from perfect themselves, those seekers feel quite frustrated because they see their problems and longings and suppose that these enlightened teachers don't have any problems any more.

TP: Problems will always be there, the difference is that after awakening, there is no longer any person having problems. Finding Liberation is not the same as being perfect. As a result, there is no test available to check if someone is enlightened. All I can say is that I can see a lot of ignorance. There is no such thing as an enlightened person because the person has to disappear first in order to let Liberation or Awakening happen. And there are no rules as to how this should happen. Again, a lot of misconceptions about all this come from the East. And a good thing happening now is that some western teachers are much more ordinary. Instead of so-called masters speaking to their followers, they are like friends sharing among friends that in fact we are all gods. Still our mind is very attached to spiritual heroes. But idolatry creates a schism in the heads of the seekers, because they realize that they can never be like their spiritual heroes. That is why I say, 'We are It, you are It.' It is also in the book *The Open Secret*: no-one is enlightened. Most seekers still believe that the gurus and awakened ones are all-knowing, all-forgiving, and in permanent bliss, and that is absolutely untrue.

JK: But why do all these masters allow their followers to say this about them? Or do people just need this kind of belief and create it for themselves?

TP: I think a lot of Eastern gurus were set up that way because they had such an immense following, a lot of people expected a lot from them, and idealized them in some way or another.

JK: Through human history, it has been happening all the time: people creating belief systems. Is it all a matter of avoiding the truth?

TP: In the end, nothing is wrong with this, it is all consciousness playing the game of a guy sitting in the front telling stories, and people sitting around him and believing him. That is how consciousness wants it![laughing]. And there is nothing you can do about it.

JK: I see.

TP: But what is interesting these days is that there are now people sitting and listening straight from the shoulder. And what consciousness is up to now is a completely different game. There are people I am talking to who are awakening to 'This' in a very simple and ordinary way.

JK: But still many people believe that you have to be *ready* for This. Isn't such a statement a reflection of a personal view, of a vision that arises out of a belief in time, out of the belief in some future event?

TP: Yes, indeed. The thing is, people are understanding what you just said. And there are people awakening to this.

JK: In Vedanta, it is often said that there is only *one conscious-ness*, but people often argue that they have a *separate consciousness*; they say they have an individual awareness because they know their own thoughts but not the thoughts of their neighbour. People believe that they have a private conscious-ness living in a separate body because they feel their own headache and not the headache of the person that is sitting in front of them. As a result, people believe that there are as many little consciousnesses as there are people walking on this planet. So they ask: how can these so-called sages of Vedanta still say that there is only one consciousness? We all experience our own body and environment in our own unique way, don't we?

TP: That subject is also in the book: your yellow on the wall is your yellow, my yellow on the wall is my yellow, and not yours. But still all is consciousness. Consciousness is living through each one of us in its own unique way. Consciousness is living through the form of Tony Parsons and Tony Parsons is in fact the Light of the creation of all that Tony Parsons is aware of. We are in fact all gods living this creation as consciousness is living through each one of us. And that is all and everything. So, I am sitting in this room, and this is the creation. There is nothing else, it is a timeless and space-less creation and it uniquely feels like Tony Parsons' creation, and that is It. And the same idea goes for you and everyone else. We are all conscious-ness living through each one of us creating a unique Tony's world, or Jan's world, and so on. The fact that you have a headache could affect me in some way or another, but that again is my creation. Your headache is yours, and I can't know or perceive what your headache is like.

JK: But still the feeling of being separate individuals originates from the fact that we feel our own body and not other people's bodies.

TP: All I can say is that once Awakening has happened, there is no longer any question of separation. There is a oneness in everything that appears in the Tony Parsons' creation. But in the Eastern tradition it is sometimes suggested that an enlightened being knows what others are thinking or sees what is happening in other people's bodies, but all that has nothing to do with true Liberation.

JK: So in fact, all we perceive is our own creation.

TP: Yes. In the end, when Awakening happens, there is no problem with what – as an individual – one should see. There is simply no separation between me and the figure over there which is called Jan. I *am* that. But saying that I am that does not necessarily therefore mean that I *know* Jan's headache. And I don't have to. It is enough that I am that. Even saying that is ridiculous: *It* is everything.

JK: I see.

TP: [laughing]: Everything is. That is Liberation.

JK: In the book *The Open Secret* you describe your walk in the park in London. How old were you?

TP: It happened at the age of 21.

JK: You write (*The Open Secret*, p.19):

> All and everything became timeless and I no longer existed. I vanished and there was no longer an experiencer. Oneness with all and everything was what happened, and an overwhelming love filled every part. … All of this happened in a timeless flash which seemed eternal.

It is obvious that this sounds like an event that happened to you. A sudden happening that changed your life dramatically, once and for all. Isn't that description again creating expectations?

TP: I know.

JK: But maybe there are other ways. When I read your book, I see exactly what you describe, but I don't see it as a single event – more as a gradual process. To me, it is more like a going in and out – or at least that is the way it seems to be – and not like some Big Bang. Sometimes I feel like a separate person and behave like that, and sometimes there is this 'seeing'. The latter is similar to being the Presence you talk about in the book; it is about recognizing the Oneness in the simplicity of everyday life. When I am in this second state – I know it is not a state, it is just a way of putting things – all the questions are completely gone.

TP: I know it is there for you.

JK: But I never experienced an event, a special state of bliss. I used to think that something was missing, but according to your vision, it is already there. All I can say is that the above-mentioned timeless moments of being go with a feeling of simplicity and inner peace. I think there are more people in a similar situation.

TP: Yes.

JK: So, even while I am identifying with the person, 'It' is still there. You say that this game – the dream that we are playing the part of being a personality – is also part of the game consciousness is playing. It is in a way, a part of the game I have to play.

TP: You see, after awakening, it is also known that it does not matter. What changes is that you are not trying to get anywhere.

JK: I seem to have moments when I feel limited, and then moments when there are no boundaries; timeless flashes of 'being All'. During these last ones, as I said before, all questions and all seeking is gone.

TP: That's it.

JK: So, it is OK. I mean: it is OK that both states are alternating

– although the second state is not a state, but something happening out of time. In fact, I see that there is no border between the two states; that was my mind imagining a border. As a result, I don't have to look for a permanent 'timeless state.'

TP [laughing]: There is nowhere to go!

JK: That sounds simple and easy.

TP: Nothing matters, everything is appropriate.

JK: So what exactly happens when I think I am no longer seeing the infinite in and around me?

TP: Well, you retract back to the separate person, to this illusion that you are limited to this Jan that is sitting here with me, drinking tea. You reintroduce your limited sense of self.

JK: So, it is again a creation of my mind.

TP: That is what is happening, and that is OK! Nothing really matters: that is what Liberation is all about!

JK: I feel that the mind has a lot of difficulty believing all this. The mind of the seeker cannot accept the idea that there is nothing to do, nothing to attain, nowhere to go. Because all these statements leave us totally hopeless.

TP: Yes, exactly. This is totally revolutionary. And it leaves us totally helpless.

JK: And it is OK accepting all this, and it is OK *not* accepting this.

TP [laughs]: It is funny, isn't it, and at the same time it is revolutionary. *This is it.* People know that. This is the only reason to be here. It's all there is.

JK: But still the mind of the so-called seeker wants to know, needs to understand, wants to have a plan, a spiritual goal. And your writings and talks are destroying all these hopes and plans, without any mercy. You say that there is nothing we can do, and a lot of seekers do have a problem with that. But I think, personally, that it can be very useful, for example, to take away some illusions.

TP: Yes, that is right.

JK: You can't bring us to this Presence, you can't give us this all-encompassing Being, but you can take away some beliefs we have. Belief systems that are standing in the way so to speak. I think you said: *understanding can bring the seeker to the river's edge.*

TP: Exactly. For example, the belief that you have to be purified first in order to be able to see This. Or that you have to go somewhere to find Liberation there.

JK: Although you say that there is nothing to do, I have to say that reading your book, listening to your talks in London and Amsterdam, gave me new insights that I didn't have before. So, there seems to be some kind of process.

TP: There is no doubt that understanding comes into this. First we have to understand, although I know people who made the leap without understanding it. As long as there is a seeker there, understanding needs to happen! If you are looking for a teacher, I say to people, 'find someone who says that you are totally helpless'. If you believe a teaching that has any sense of having to do something, you are back in the wheel.

JK: If a teacher says that you have to do this or have to do that in order to become enlightened, the seeker is turning around in circles again, like a donkey following the carrot on the stick.

TP: Exactly. Until you find out that you are both the carrot and the stick and all the rest. One of the functions of my teaching is destroying belief systems, and leaving people totally helpless and in a position where they might say to themselves, 'I am totally helpless, what is there?' and what they may realize is 'there is This'. It is a very strange thing: this teaching is totally destructive and yet it is introducing people to the most beautiful love affair they can ever have because *they give up*. When they give up, it becomes possible that they fall in love with 'This'. When they fall in love with This, they have *everything*! That is

It. And because This never falls away, it is beyond everything. The invitation is always there, in whatever we perceive; it can never escape us.

JK: But seekers expect the invitation rather in the extraordinary than in the ordinary. We all want an invitation to the infinite in bliss but, as I understand it, it must be equally available in anger, in fear. We all want to recognize Oneness in the silence of meditation or in the beauty of the sunset, but It is also there in pain, in stress and in problems.

TP: Yes, exactly. One of the things that amazed me in the park – or afterwards, I suppose – was that I was so to speak *surrounded* by It. That we are It, everything is It! 'This' never goes away. The invitation is always there.

JK: In the book you suggest that we have to wake up: we need to wake up from the dream that we are separate entities. This is exactly the opposite of what common sense tells us about the world. Common sense says that we are all people living on a planet. Everybody knows that, except maybe a few patients living in a mental hospital. It is a worldwide accepted theory that we are all separate human beings walking around this planet, living in a body. I have tried to find someone living in my body, but unfortunately, I haven't found anybody.

TP [laughing]: Oh really.

JK [pointing at his own body]: Yes, I did try and look for someone here, but couldn't find anyone. Still I know I look like a person *to others*.

TP: Well, what my workshops are about is something similar. People are invited to have a look for that person in there. And it is possible at some point or another that they end up finding that there is nobody there. All this Jan who is sitting there is pure awareness. And that is all there is.

JK: That sounds a bit like we are becoming insane.

TP [laughing]: Yes, exactly: it is complete madness.

JK: Maybe it is so mad that even the psychiatrists will not understand us.

TP [seriously]: And it has happened at several times that people really see that.

JK: See what?

TP: It happens during the talks and workshops that people see that actually *there is nobody there*. And that can happen quite gently, that people come to See. What they realize is that what they are is pure awareness. I ask questions like, 'Are you the mind?', 'Are you in the body?'. And then people come to a blank wall; there is nothing there. Then I ask them, 'Where are you now?' and 'Stay there; what is it like?'.

JK: Just as simple as that; until they find out that there is nobody there.

TP: And it may sound as a process, but it is not. It is timeless.

JK: So, you invite people in your workshops to leave all ambition, and discover that there is no-one there. But if there is nothing to do, nothing to achieve, nowhere to go, why should we read your book, why should we attend your talks or workshops? Isn't it a paradox, saying to people that there is nothing to do, and at the same time organizing lectures?

TP: Yes, it is. People say to me in the talks: when there is no purpose, what are we doing here? I say to them, 'You sit here, and the only thing you can do is discover there is nothing you can do'. That is a discovery! If consciousness chooses you to sit here, you will be sitting here.

JK: Another thing is people being jealous about you, especially when they are reading the text in the book where you describe when It happened to you while walking in that park in London. When seekers read this part of your book, they may say to themselves, 'Tony has found something that I don't have, and I want it too. So, I will go and see him.'

TP: I know.

JK: People think to themselves: he has become a special being that I am *not yet*, and they say, 'I want to be like him; being liberated like him will solve all my problems'. People are expecting a lot from this Liberation. This in fact also creates a kind of craving, a spiritual goal, that people will try and imitate you. As a result, those seekers want the same state that you seem to have. But I suppose it doesn't work that way, does it?

TP: No, not at all. What I say to people is that they should not wait for some event. That Liberation is not something that I have and that they don't have. And although it may sound spectacular, it doesn't have to be that way, although it can. It is rather simple than special. For some people it comes gradually, and one day they find out they are already there. It has happened that way to several people I know.

JK: But most seekers are waiting for something spectacular to happen, they have read that Liberation is a sudden and complete transformation in an almost divine state of bliss and perfect happiness. As a result, many seekers – since they know they don't have any special experience that lasts for ever – are frustrated. Or they feel as if they have failed in some way or another. Or they had a glimpse of 'It' once, but never got it back again, and they are still desperately seeking.

TP: I know.

JK: They read the right books, they do their meditation, they eat and behave the right way, they go and see the masters, without finding Liberation. And when you tell them it is simple and obvious, and that there is nothing to do to find Liberation, that becomes even more frustrating for them.

TP: Well, maybe there would be less confusion if I had left the chapter that describes my walk in the park out of the book. In the newest version of the book (1999) a new chapter called 'I am' is added, which deals with this subject. It says that *no conditions need to be fulfilled* (p. 47).

JK: It is a lovely chapter, indeed. You state that this Liberation is so simple, that waking up is something *anyone* can have, without any effort or belief. If you said that it was difficult, something to be obtained only after many years of meditation or spiritual practice, at least that would leave the reader with something to *do*, some kind of goal, some kind of homework. But as I said before, you don't give any of these; you leave the reader without any homework, without any hope.

TP: One of the things that I say to people is: don't look for a goal, even don't look for the non-doer. You don't even have to be purified first in order to become worthy for Liberation. Liberation brings with it the realization that there is no-one to liberate.

JK: It is obvious that we can have a Western life, and still see the invitation of the infinite. We can drink wine, have a house, have a family life, and so on. We don't have to meditate twice a day, we don't have to go and live in an ashram in India to become enlightened one day. There are no conditions. In other words: there are no rules.

TP: Exactly: everybody is in a perfect position to wake up: the invitation is always there. It is available right now, while we are having tea. But the mind is always creating avoidance, and the mind is very clever at that. And finally, the latter is also the infinite expression playing its game.

JK: So, in the end, nothing is wrong with the mind, nothing is wrong with seekers thinking that they are limited, believing that they have to do specific things or behave in certain ways in order to become worthy for this. Finally, nothing is wrong with people who believe that holistic therapy or spiritual practice will bring them Liberation, or at least prepare them for It.

TP: As I said before, everything is appropriate. It is all the infinite expression. There is no reason to fight the ego, to suppress the thinking mind, to look for the ego-less state, which is again very Eastern. There is actually nothing wrong with the mind, with the ego: it is all part of the game [laughing].

JK: Therapy and meditation are also part of the game, doing yoga and looking for moments of bliss, fighting against our dark sides, and so on: these are also an expression of consciousness.

TP [seriously]: But *it is not what you are.*

JK: Still, the seeker is left with a paradox, realizing that the ego cannot chase itself away. When I took the train from Brussels to London yesterday, I saw an advertisement for a product to stop smoking. It said, 'Don't quit quitting.' Isn't that the same paradox that seekers are encountering when they are told that they have to stop the thinking mind, while *trying to stop* is also part of the thinking mind? It is like looking for the ego-less state: who is there to look for the ego-less state but the ego? How can we quit thinking? How can one part of the ego chase the other part away? How can the ego chase itself away? Isn't that impossible? Doesn't it all come to suicide?

TP: Yes, exactly: it is all about suicide. But on the other hand, there is no need to kill the ego, there is no need to look for the ego-less state: that is all a mind game. It is a battle you create that keeps the mind game going. The so-called 'great battle between good and evil'.

JK: In Amsterdam you said that physical death is also complete Liberation. Does that imply that suicide is the fastest way to enlightenment?

TP. Well, physical death is indeed complete Liberation. People return to what they are, which is consciousness. They are back home. Of course, it is not you going back home, you are already home anyway.

JK: Still, all these belief systems say that there is a soul going somewhere after you die. Many people have reported seeing themselves lying on the ground in a near-death experience. I used to believe in some sort of afterlife myself, although I realized I could never prove the existence of it. But since I read Ramesh Balsekar, Douglas Harding and Tony Parsons, a lot of belief systems have evaporated.

TP: I see.

JK: But many seekers do believe in an afterlife. A lot of people hope that their higher self will go to some place in the galaxy – or in another dimension – to wait there in a process of transformation, in order to come back to earth to reincarnate, or to go to heaven or hell.

TP: That is all rubbish, of course. You know that, Jan: it all comes down to the belief in the self. And the mind will try to find any way in which it can continue after death. So, the mind will create several scenarios for the idea to continue in some form or another.

JK: And religious organizations have only stimulated these belief systems about what happens after we die.

TP: But the truth is that when you die, *it is just over:* the novel is over.

JK: Does it mean that the light is just turned off?

TP: It is consciousness manifesting, and then being still.

JK: So, the idea of a soul is our creation, because we are afraid of dying. And similarly, the hope of reincarnation is a reflection of our fear of physical death. People are simply afraid of disappearing forever, and their minds just make up the rest. Our minds create stories that suggest that we survive after physical death, that we continue.

TP: Yes, indeed. But there is no soul: it is just a belief system.

JK: But at the same time, it is true in a way for those who believe in it.

TP: Yes it is. When you look at most belief systems, they actually last *as long as you believe in them.* You can believe you have a soul for five minutes, then five minutes later you believe that you are angry with your wife, and so on.

JK: You mean that they exist as long as they are there as belief systems.

TP: People put such an investment in belief systems. For example, 'I believe in karma, I believe in an afterlife', and that is how it seems as long as you believe in it. At that moment, it is what it is. But five minutes later… it is gone! [laughs] It is wonderful, isn't it?

JK: Yes.

TP [very enthusiastic]: Isn't it stunning? It is stunning, isn't it? There is a guy who was at one of our meetings – maybe he will be in the workshop today – he is a gardener, actually, and he suddenly woke up to this 'Thing of Creation' and how we are all creating different realities at every moment, and he said, 'Tony, I am absolutely stunned with the genius of Consciousness.'

JK: It is a wonder, indeed. Each of us creating his own little world. And we don't need to imagine a higher being for that. We don't have to create a personal projection, a god standing behind or above this creation. There is no need for something higher that manages or creates all this. Many people seem to feel the need for such a higher intelligence. They strongly believe in the existence of such a being.

TP: Forget it!

JK: But people seem to need the belief in that higher genius.

TP: I know, but there really is no need for a higher being above us. We *are* the genius!

JK: Yes!

TP [laughing]: *We* are doing it right now! Isn't it amazing?

JK: It is wonderful.

TP [seriously]: When one knows that one is *this*, there is a delight, and a deep gratitude.

JK: Oh, yes. I see what you mean. Then there is no more than *this*, just this Presence, as you call it in your book. Then, all questions are gone; at least, that is the way I see it. No more books, no more talks, everything is as it is.

TP: You see, as you are opening your mouth and asking a question, that is It. *That is It*. You know, as you sit and listen to the answer, that's It. Just bringing you back to *This* is so fundamental.

JK: And that is what the workshops are about.

TP: Exactly.

JK: Tony, do you enjoy doing this, sharing this vision with people?

TP: I don't know why I am doing it, but there is a joy in sharing this, indeed. And during the talks, there is more going on than just talking, there is more than just questions and answers. It is a sharing; it is not just me sitting there and others listening to me.

The other thing about the talks I give is that I have absolutely no investment in results. I am not trying to sell anything, I am not interested in the effects. We are just sitting together in a room. So there is no sense of 'I have failed or succeeded' because there is nobody there to fail or succeed.

JK: And there is no judgement.

TP: And there is no such thing as failure or success. If someone at the end of a workshop goes away saying, 'I didn't get anything out of it' or 'that was awful', then that is it.

JK: That sounds quite liberating, because you don't feel any pressure on you or on your workshops. Maybe those who come to the workshops should have the same attitude. Many seekers have a lot of expectations, especially when they go and see someone who is said to be awakened.

TP: If a so-called teacher has an investment in what he is saying, forget about it. In the end, everything is appropriate. All that is happening is pure awareness manifesting.[51]

I sometimes say at the beginning of a workshop that I don't know what is going to happen. All I can say is that I suggest people try and drop all expectation. All we do is just celebrate being here. We just look at 'what is here', and see behind this 'where am I in what is here'. What we are from this perspective is pure awareness. We are the light that allows perceptions to come up and disappear again. No questions about it, no analysis of it, no judgement about what arises. Whatever happens, happens. Including the sense of being the self, including the belief systems.

JK: Finally, we are back where we came from. Which reminds me of the last sentence of that chapter 'I am' in your book. There you say:

> I don't even have to wait for grace to descend.
> For I am, you are, it is already the abiding grace. (p.48)

You are space for my face

INTERVIEW WITH DOUGLAS HARDING, LOUVAIN
(BELGIUM), 09.03.2000

JK: It is about 60 years now that you have been around to share your vision. How did it all get started?

DH: I was 31 years old when the penny dropped, the so-called Himalayan experience. It is described in the book *On Having No Head*. But instead of 'seeing this' in the mountains, it could have happened anywhere; it has nothing to do with the mountains.

JK: Although that Himalayan experience may sound to some readers like a peak experience, it was not really that special, was it?

DH: Well, it is not something special at all, but rather something *natural*. This is something that – when you see it – connects with everything. It is the revelation of the obvious, not the achievement of the extraordinary.

JK: It is not some kind of peak experience but rather a *valley* experience.

DH: Yes, exactly; it is not a mystical experience.

JK: Still, many people have a lot of expectations about this. They don't know the difference between awakening and bliss.

DH: Oh, yes, absolutely. One of the ways to avoid seeing 'This' is by projecting it into peak experiences.

JK: You said today that since you first saw It 60 years ago, it developed through the years. What do you mean by that?

DH: Well, you have to be careful about this. And distinguish between what develops and what does not develop. There is a sudden aspect and a gradual aspect; the sudden aspect is that once you see It, this is it. The gradual aspect is that there is a development of what I would call 'continuity' and also a development of trust. The first one – seeing who you are – is always the same, the second one is a gradual thing.

JK: Can you explain this?

DH: Well, the vision is the same, the same, the same. Why? Because it is simple and clear, and Clarity is Clarity is Clarity. And it is not spotty at times or only half a clarity. *This* remains always the same. What does change – in my experience – are two things. One is the *continuity* of the vision; at first it is flashing in and out, you always have to come back to it [points with his finger at his face[52]]. The second one is a matter of *trust*. You don't trust It in the beginning, you don't trust It to run your life. But one learns to trust this Clarity. So gradually there is a development of continuity and a development of trust. This is a very gradual thing. So in the end, it all becomes *natural*.

JK: So, as one practises it, it becomes more and more natural; and as a result we don't need the experiments any more.[53]

DH: Exactly! And as one practises it – and it has to be practised by always coming back from appearance to reality, by making this journey – it is happening more and more naturally.

JK: Is it becoming like an automatic process.

DH: Yes, you're right. But I don't know if 'automatic' is the right word. I still feel that it becoming natural is on account of you practising it. By just coming back to the place you never left. At least, that is my impression. One just comes back to what we are looking out of.

JK: I can see your face over there, I see you drinking tea, and I can see my Clarity 'here', without having to do the pointing experience. It is there all the time, and so is this 'Space' here.

DH: You are Space for my face, you are Capacity for it.

JK: All the time.

DH: All the time. In fact, you don't need an experiment to see this.[54]

JK: How does this seeing relate to religion?

DH: When we talk about religion, we must distinguish between the heart of the matter and the popular version of each religion. You know that I have been writing and teaching about comparing the great religions of the world. My discovery is that the heart of each of the great religions is one simple proposition: that central to all sentient beings is *the One Awareness in all beings*. So whatever one's religious background, so whatever your religious belief, what you will find in the heart of that religion, is exactly the same Awareness we are talking about in the workshops and in my books.

JK: So it perfectly fits with whatever belief you were brought up in, be it Christianity, Buddhism, Islam, Hinduism, and so on.

DH: I was brought up in Christianity. For me, Christianity has something very special at its root and heart: it says that the power behind the world is self-giving love, and that is to me the ultimate revelation. And that is exactly what we have discovered today in the experiments. When you are in the paper tube, you are disappearing in favour of your friend who is sitting in front of you. Seeing that you are *built* this way, built wide open to love one another, that is what it is all about. But this has nothing to do with my emotions or feelings. I am not talking about romantic love or sentimental feelings.

JK: Is it more like *impersonal* love?

DH: Yes. It is completely disappearing for the other, it is really dying for the other. At this moment, I found that Douglas has disappeared in favour of Jan. I have 'nothing' here [pointing at his face] and I have over there the appearance of that man called

'Jan'. It is not happening because I am a nice chap, but because I am *built* that way.

JK: It is like exchanging faces. You have my face, and I have yours.

DH: Trading faces. That is what I call it.

JK: And the timeless background is always there. It is *out of time*, so to speak.

DH: Yes.

JK: Before I discovered your experiments, I read a lot of books about Zen Buddhism, Taoism and Vedanta. These books say exactly the same thing. They all talk about unconditional love, about dying for the other, about resurrection, about the fact that what we really are is the One Consciousness. But I thought at the time I understood what it was all about until I did this pointing experiment and tunnel experiment for the first time. Although it was just a flash of 'naked being' at the time, I knew immediately that I was onto something extremely important. I was given a glimpse of something I was longing for all my life. Not a blissful state – although it tasted blissful – but rather the most simple thing I had ever seen.

DH: I know what you mean.

JK: What changed after getting into this seeing more deeply – if I can put it that way – is that I noticed to my surprise that the same books I was reading now became obvious and simple. Discovering that really was a revelation. I really *saw* what it was all about, I recognized the same Truth, that same awareness in different traditions, approached in a variety of ways by different teachers. I also noticed a lot of ignorance, or sidetracks so to speak, and I was given a 'vision' that brought me straight to the heart of the matter. And so I must say that your experiments gave me the *practical* approach about something that before was always covered by words, by concepts.

DH: It is practical, indeed.

JK: Once you have 'seen' this, you start recognizing this same truth in completely different approaches. Words can never describe this 'One Awareness' but only point at it.

DH: And you see, what you said Jan is so true: there are a million miles between real spiritual life and *knowing* all about it. You can be a professor in religion or philosophy, you may know all the rules about loving the neighbour as yourself, but as long as you don't 'see' it, it is just a concept. You may know all the scriptures, and still be a million miles away from the core.

JK: It is about *being* it, not knowing it.

DH: Exactly.

JK: Is discovering this seeing more about becoming ordinary instead of being special?

DH: It makes you more ordinary than special. You don't feel special. I think this is very important because this seeing has nothing to do with a guru and disciples. I don't behave like that because *I don't feel like that.* When you really see who you really are, you see you are No-thing, and so *you are not superior.* The fact that you wish to celebrate it, and share it with friends, that is your privilege. But it doesn't mean that other people aren't there, they are all in a certain sense enlightened. They are just ignorant about their own enlightenment. So you can't feel superior. It is very democratic, this vision.

JK: It has nothing to do with one person being better or more spiritual than the other.

DH: The word enlightenment is a dirty word because it has been misused. I don't use it in the workshops. The sentence 'I am enlightened and you are endarkened' just won't do. It doesn't work that way.

JK: Your message is completely different.

DH: I say, 'This is obvious, this is sharable.' My story is about sharing this. It is good news. It is not about superiority. If someone is interested ...

JK: ... you are open and available.

DH: That's right. I invite people to discover for themselves who they are.

JK: Why is there still so much confusion about this? Why are there still so many masters around; why are their followers pretending that their guru is having special powers? Why do people want to become devotees, rather than just investigators?

DH: Well, you see, Jan, we have a huge resistance to 'This'. Why? Well, because it is death. And although it is immediately followed by resurrection, people are afraid of 'It'. We all have this resistance − including Douglas − and one form that this resistance takes is *creating a distance*, by imagining this spiritual search. People go and see a guru, who is so-called enlightened, and they say, 'He is all the way there, and I am halfway there, and he will help me in this journey'. People say, 'I am a seeker', and don't realize that at the same time they secretly say to themselves, 'I am sure *I will not be a finder*'. Seekers are terrified to be a finder. And while being a seeker, while following the path, you have all the rewards of being on a spiritual journey without the danger − in fact, the lethal danger − of arrival. Because arrival is death, and it is resurrection. People simply don't see that.

JK: Is it the same fear that prevents people 'seeing the One Consciousness' during the experiments?

DH: Exactly. Many people do think they don't 'see' it, but I think one has to see it first before one can reject it; we see it so briefly but unconsciously we reject it immediately. I think it is impossible *not to see it*.

JK: But still many people complain that they seem to miss the point of your experiments.

DH: People have so many excuses to avoid it: they say they don't understand it, that they expected something far more spectacular, that they don't see the point of it, or they just fall asleep. It is all the same avoidance, the same fear for this 'No-thing', that same fear of disappearing.

JK: And we have to accept that phenomenon of resistance. When the electric current is too strong, I think it is better to use one's safety fuses than to have a complete short circuit of the nervous system. Maybe this avoidance is just a mechanism of self-protection. Something people use 'when they are not ready yet'.

DH: Catherine and I go around the world giving workshops, and we know that it is only a small proportion of people who really see it. But with the years, the group is growing, and the seeds will germinate when the time has come.

JK: I think there is also a joy in sharing this.

DH: Oh very much. Absolutely.

JK: It is one of the most beautiful things we can ever share with someone, isn't it?

DH: It is *the* most valuable one.

JK: And still many people don't 'get it'.

DH: It's a mystery. We don't know who is ready and who is not. In the group of 80 people we had here today in Belgium, maybe a few, three, four or five, will really get it and have their lives changed.

JK: Don't you think that more people are 'open' to this kind approach than ever before?

DH: Well, Jan, it seems to me – not because of Douglas but in spite of Douglas – that this is a spiritual breakthrough in history because the experiments turn 'hear-say' into 'look-see' and that is revolutionary. It is amazing that during the last 5,000 years nobody insisted on looking just 'here' [pointing at his face], just turning the attention 180 degrees.

JK: It is like putting all the theory into practice.

DH: This is where the Dzochgen fits in so nicely, 'Seeing with naked awareness'. It is obvious, natural, and everyone has it.

JK: And it is simple.

DH: And it is shareable. And also totally neglected. I think that the time has come to let it come to the surface, now. You see, in the past only a few people came through to this beatific vision. You had masses of people who were on the road, seeking, but only a few realized absolute union with God. I think that now more people will come to this.

JK: But you don't suggest that it is only for the happy few.

DH: In a certain sense, you just become like a child again, which is like what Jesus said – 'Unless you become like a little child, you will never enter the Kingdom of Heaven.'

JK: If you had to sum up your message to people who are not familiar with your workshops and books, what would you say?

DH: I can sum it up in seven words, 'I am not what I look like'. I am the opposite of what I look like. You got *what I look like*, I got *what I am*. And what I am looking out of is different from what I am looking at in the mirror. When I look in the mirror, that is what I am looking at, but what I am looking out of is *Space*. Total difference, in every respect. I appear to be a solid lump, but 'here' I am transparent: again, a total difference. I appear to be looking out of two eyes, while 'here' there is only one eye.

JK: This vision is at the same time so simple and at the same time so profound. It is a paradox: it is changing everything, without actually changing anything. Nothing needs to be changed in order to see 'This'.

DH: Profound things are simple. If it is not simple, it cannot be true. But simple things are difficult.

JK: People prefer complicated theories.

DH: Mankind hates simplicity.

JK: Making it complicated is another way of avoiding 'It'.

DH: What you do is *wake up* to things, not changing events; you just 'awake' to them. It is not about engineering the world we are in.

JK: Is it true that this vision helps you to accept things as they are, that you are less tempted to change things?

DH: There is a paradox here. You are quite right. Catherine and I don't say we want to change the world into Utopia. That is not going to happen because that is impossible. Our chief concern is not changing the world, our concern is sharing this vision of the world *from its Source*. Although it is not aimed at changing the world, it is the profoundest change that has ever been engineered.

JK: It really is the profoundest change that can happen.

DH: When the Buddha was enlightened, it necessarily meant the enlightenment of all sentient beings. And the Buddha couldn't be enlightened without involving the enlightenment of all sentient beings. Because only the One can be enlightened, and not Jan or Douglas.

JK: A lot of seekers think that as long as the ego is standing in the way, enlightenment is not possible. That it is impossible to see this Transparency as long as we identify with the ego.

DH: I don't know how I have to put this. [silence] I am simply noticing at this moment that 'here' there is Space, and 'over there' there are chairs and windows. Here is just emptiness. There is no getting my ego out of the way, and all that stuff. There is just the seeing, shining in great brilliance and clarity; I am not attacking the 'little one'. The person 'here' disappears in favour of what happens around me, and that is all there is, really. It is absolutely unbelievable. Here everything is on display, with absolutely nothing standing in its way. If I waited until the disappearance of the little ego called Douglas Harding for seeing 'This', I would still be waiting for it. [Laughter]

JK: So there is no need to forget the ego and its mechanisms.

DH: I don't like to use the word 'ego'. I don't know what an ego really is. It seems to me to be a concept we just play games

with. I don't talk in terms of abstractions, but in terms of experiments, like for example a finger pointing to this No-thing.
My business is to trade in concepts for what I call 'percepts'.
But again, let's be careful with words. If I would like to give a
message to the readers of this interview, I would like to ask
them 'to do something' and not just *read* this.

JK: You don't want them to create new concepts. Or to just
think about what we have been saying here.

DH: Exactly.

DH: So let's not end the text of this interview on a concept
or an idea. Let's end on something the readers have to *do*.

JK: That may be the final message of this conversation: to put
things into practice right away.

DH: To the reader of this interview, I would like to say, 'You
see the black marks on the white paper you are about to read
just now, and I invite you strongly to just see *what is taking it in*'.
That is what it is all about. See who or rather what is looking.
It is the Space that is taking it all in. That is the point, that is
the situation or vision I want to share: what you are *looking at*
is printed words, what you are *looking out of* is Space for them.

JK: And that is not a theory, that is just seeing what we are,
right now.

DH: Yes.

JK: Thank you, Douglas, for this interview. It was a joy to have
this conversation, and to notice your enthusiasm. And to share
this vision. Thanks again.

DH: The pleasure was all mine.

Beyond masculine and feminine

SECOND INTERVIEW WITH TONY PARSONS, LONDON, 18.3.2000

JK: In the train, I was reading a few chapters of your book *The Open Secret* and I came upon this part where you write [p. 14]: *I was fascinated and frightened of women*. Do you want to talk about that, or do you think it is too personal a matter for an interview?

TP: I don't mind talking about this subject, and I am sure I will be talking for an awful lot of men. First I want to say this: I don't think that there is anything like a woman or a man, I think there is just energy that is feminine or male. I think what frightens male energy in female energy is the thing of 'giving up'.

JK: They are afraid of letting go.

TP: It is frightening to some men, at least. And that is one of the reasons why religion has been so influenced by the patriarchy the last two thousand years. Men, and especially priests – both from the Eastern as from the Western traditions – are so frightened of feminine energy because it represents actually a kind of fire, a sort of aliveness, a kind of chaos, and men basically want to be *in control*. Masculine energy wants to be in control and the female energy threatens that. That is why women must be kept at a distance.

JK: You think that is why men and women are separated in temples and monasteries? And why women are not allowed at certain levels of religious organization? You think that is why the Pope and the Dalai Lama and the great Zen masters were all men, and have never been surrounded by or actually living with women? Why priests in general always avoid contact with women? And why they projected that concept onto the rest of the population, for example by saying that physical pleasure is bad for us? That sex is dangerous for our spiritual growth?

TP: You see, intuition and the 'fire' of woman represents that thing that the male can be frightened of. But man also is fascinated by it, of course. Because the man – or the male energy – also wants to give up and be lost.

JK: It is a paradox: on the one hand, man wants to be in control, and on the other hand, he wants to lose himself in the fire of the female.

TP: Exactly. Man also wants to be lost, indeed. Wants to give up completely, but at the same time he is frightened of it because it feels like dying.

JK: I like your expression of 'being lost'.

TP: Someone said, 'I would like to be lying shipwrecked between your thighs.'

JK: That expresses exactly what I wanted to say: losing yourself in the arms of your lover.

TP: There are many moments in making love when there is no one there.

JK: That is what it is all about.

TP: A relationship that has a lot of energy can bring along things in you that point to … something else. It is not *another* dimension I am referring to, but that which has no dimensions. As I said before, an interaction between two people can cause a movement in ourselves towards 'something else'.

JK: It is about a movement which can bring us to rediscovering our true identity.

TP: About getting lost.

JK: You may remember when you were reading an early version of my book *Coming Home*,[55] that I mention this in several chapters. For example, realizing that there is nobody inside our body, and that it can be a wonderful and beautiful way of discovering that through love play.

TP: Yes.

JK: I think it is a wonderful and easy way of disappearing. Suddenly, you are 'gone'.

TP: Exactly. It is wonderful, isn't it?

JK: Yes, it is. But it is not always like that, for most people, I mean. Or it is not always like that in a specific relationship.

TP: Osho used to say, 'The problem with a man and a woman making love is that four people get into the bed. There are two bodies and two minds.' Then, nothing much is happening. It is just an activity.

JK: Just some friction between two bodies.

TP: That's right.

JK: And not a disappearing for each other.

TP: But on the other hand, some people discover that there is another way of meeting one another. There come moments when the energy between the two people is really powerful, where one is lost.

JK: It is like an ice cube disappearing in water.

TP: And I think especially men are afraid of that; that is what I was pointing at in *The Open Secret* when I said I was afraid of women.

JK: Well, it is said that you just have to lose your head: just cut of your head and put it beside the bed, on the side table, and then just go for it. [laughter] It is all about putting away the thinking mind. Forgetting about the mind that wants to control.

TP: Yes, it is. There is indeed a kind of energy that can appear when a man and a woman meet; sometimes it is not happening, or with some people it is not happening …

JK: And even that is OK. It may not appear when you meet one person and then it happens with someone else. It is a mystery.

TP: And I can see so many hang-ups being exposed through a relationship of a man and a woman.

JK: What do you mean by that?

TP: I think when you are in a relationship with somebody and there really is this 'energy' there, somehow everything comes out. It is either that, or one has to put it away. When people in some way or another decide to 'put away things', the relation becomes a relation of *agreement*. Then, things are hidden.

JK: You mean that certain subjects or certain aspects of the relationships are just put under the carpet?

TP: Both partners agree that they will not go into certain areas, and then nothing really is happening any more.

JK: It is like two dead people living together.

TP: That is one way you can go. The other way you can go is not hiding anything for each other. And that can really be an explosion.

JK: But the problem then may be that people are turning all this into a technique. I mean, people start to read books about Tantra and try to copy techniques. They feel frustrated that their current relationship is not as explosive as it should be, and they try to do something about it. They buy the right books and try to imitate the descriptions by learning some so-called Tantric techniques.

TP: Special techniques or looking for ecstatic experiences has nothing to do with 'Liberation'. And still it is all appropriate.

JK: A problem I think with trying the Tantric techniques is that the popular books are not the same as the original 'message'. Similar to what happened with traditional religion, the initial authentic experience – if I can use such a description – is overshadowed by what has been said about it afterwards.

TP: Yes.

JK: Imagine the difference between what Jesus really said and really wanted to say to his close friends, and what we are hearing twenty centuries later. Imagine the difference between what Buddha really said and really wanted to say, and what we are reading about Buddhism right now.

TP: I know.

JK: I suppose it is the same with Tantra. The authentic shift of disappearing for one another cannot be achieved by a technique, by trying to experience something from a personal point of view.

TP: You mention that in your book, don't you?

JK: I try to do so. Quite easily, people get into a technique again, trying to control things, trying to 'get it' while there is exactly nobody there to get it. They are looking for an experience.

TP: Yes, indeed.

JK: I think it is not a matter of a technique, it is not a matter of a person getting somewhere, but just a matter of letting it happen, of rediscovering the most simple aspects of our beingness. When you look at the face of your partner, it is just a matter of noticing our true identity: 'I have a clarity 'here' and I see your face 'there' and *what I am* is space for your appearance.' That's all. What we really are is this Clarity, which is Consciousness.

TP: Yes. As simple as that.

JK: It doesn't have to be in the form of orgasmic explosions or exclusive mystical peak experiences; it may be happening while there is a very simple way of communicating between two lovers, while there is just a gentle contact between one body part and another one. Without any pillow-book technique. Without trying to control anything. Without the flowers, candles and the incense. Without reaching out for something spectacular.

TP: Yes, that is so ...

JK: Just a very simple touch ... No need to control anything.

TP: I know.

JK: It can happen *without* the Kundalini, *without* the cosmic energy. It is so simple ... just disappearing ... it is wonderful. All the rest – the energies, the ecstasies – may be there, of course, nothing is wrong *if* it happens, but none of it is essential. And they are not goals to be striving for.

TP: When it happens, it is a very powerful situation in which that 'letting go' can arise. No control. But the mind will even turn this into a process, and there are teachers who recommend so-called 'divine sex' as a way to awakening. I see many people who are damaged by trying to aspire to this kind of ignorance.

JK: I think that is also one of the characteristics of the message of your book *The Open Secret* when you talk about presence, about discovering what we really are: 'no control'. It all has to do with *simplicity*. Your book was the first one I read that put it so clearly. We don't have to change anything, we don't have to become better in any sense, because It is already there. I am sure other writers are pointing at the same thing, but they never actually got it so simple and clear.

TP: It is revolutionary, in a way. And again: extremely simple.

JK. But there is also a lot of interpretation going on. The initial 'truth' being altered.

TP: Yes. It is true.

JK: Why are people making things complicated? Why are we avoiding this simplicity?

TP: We don't know why we are creating avoidance. And at the same time – somewhere – we *know*. Somewhere we have this intelligence that something is real and something is not. Once that starts to emerge, you have a *filter*, and you filter out what is artificial and you know what is genuine. Then there is a sort of resonance, and that can also happen when meeting people.

JK: But on the other hand, you said before that you also saw a lot of ignorance. And a lot of people seem to be attracted by that. Teachers who 'sell' a popular story, who promise personal salvation, who pretend that their energy can bring other people to a higher level of consciousness, and all that sort of thing: they seem to be very popular. They are much more popular than someone like you who is saying that there is nowhere to go. That there is no hope, that everything is just happening. It is not very popular to say that there is no life-story, no future, that people have no past nor present.

TP: Yes, a lot of people don't stay around me for long.

JK: People seem to be more attracted to charismatic teachers, or simply to those gurus who tell their students exciting stories. Maybe seekers don't want to hear the 'naked truth'. Am I wrong if I have the impression that in those cases seekers get the resonance with the *wrong* energies, so to speak?

TP: It is more that people are very *excited* by all these stories, they are very excited *emotionally* by what appears to be very powerful. Being with a charismatic guru can be very exciting. And I am not suggesting that it is completely wrong, it even may seem to be genuine for a while, but it is only so at a certain level. Not at a very deep level. And it often creates dependency.

JK: The ego needs sensation. Wants to know things, feel things. People want to admire heroes in this case: they want to meet spiritual heroes and imitate them, just like teenagers imitate their pop stars. But it is not always like that; some seekers really want to know, don't they? People who want to get to the bottom line.

TP: Yes, indeed, and sooner or later they will discover It in the simplicity of what is. I meet several people like that in my meetings. People who really want to know. You see, underneath this longing for sensation there is another level. There is a 'deeper' resonance that knows that there is a deeper sense of simplicity that runs all this.

JK: But nobody ever told me that *so clearly.* I had to wait for your book to really realize that simplicity, that immediateness. I know I have read it before, in other books I mean, but it never was made clear to me. Or maybe I was – as they say sometimes – not ready yet. Not ready yet for seeing this simplicity. Reading your book, I finally found someone who had written down what I was suspecting all the time. It was quite a relief to find out I was not the only one. A recognition of what I knew already. Some childlike openness that I knew was whispering to me deep inside.

TP: This is it.

JK: Still there are a lot of teachers or masters who are very serious about what they are saying, who are still going around and sort of 'personalize' enlightenment.

TP: I realized recently that a lot of so-called teachers had some kind of *experience,* something that really has happened to them, but what has not happened to them is the *clarity.* They don't know how to communicate It in a clear and uncompromised way. Their teaching is still personalized.

JK: Exactly!

TP: They are still going around teaching, without having the clarity.

JK: For me, that is a unique situation in *your* conversations: I see someone who is talking about this in a direct, simple and clear way. And now I realize it: It is right here, while I am sitting in this chair. I don't need you any more to see that. It is all there. We don't have to leave this hotel and go somewhere to find it.

TP: Yes.

JK: Even when I am frustrated because I am stuck in a traffic jam, It is still there. Normally, such moments are regarded as 'non-spiritual' and not 'yogi-like'. For example, yoga teachers feel very frustrated about all this: about having to admit that they have their moments of so-called negative emotions. They are never supposed to be jealous or angry, for example.

TP: Oh yes.

JK: I realize now that these moments of so-called negative emotions will always be appearing. There is nothing I can change about that. What can change is that there is nobody there any more who is frustrated about these negative emotions.

TP: Yes.

JK: So now I just don't care any more; it is what it is. Presence is equally available when we are in a bad mood.

TP: Exactly.

JK: In that way, this vision has a kind of 'practical value', although I know that is absolutely unimportant. Life just flows more easily, that's all. I know it sounds like it is a personal achievement, but I didn't mean it that way. Let me put it this way: we just seem to invest less energy into *resistance*.

TP: It is revolutionary, actually.

JK: Yes. Seeing this is really changing *everything*, and at the same time everything remains the same. And we don't have to do anything to 'obtain' this insight.

TP: Many teachers still say that you have to be or behave in a certain way. Basically, they all come back to the mind; the mind is making a discipline out of it. Or the mind is getting it organized in a religion or a community. It is all a very masculine approach, I think. Over the last 2,000 years, it has been approached in a very masculine way, but recently it has been changing.

JK: Into a more feminine direction?

TP: Well, I would rather say a marriage between both. Or if you like, beyond both masculine and feminine. But it has nothing to do with feminism.

JK: A kind of equilibrium. With less need for control and rules.

TP: Before I wrote the book *The Open Secret* and started to give lectures and intensives, I had been seeing several people talking about my discovery in the park, about my vision. I talked with them on an individual basis. One of the things I said to them was, 'There are no rules', you don't have to be a vegetarian or be celibate, all of that is an avoidance of this *as it is*. Actually it is all manipulation.

JK: It is avoidance.

TP: When you say that to people, it is wonderful: you see people suddenly blossoming, they just let go.

JK: They suddenly realize that there can't be any rules when we are talking about the One, when we are aiming at non-dualism. They are glad to realize that the religious leaders were wrong when they suggested that sex is bad, and designed strictly for procreation. They suddenly realize that all the rules really don't matter.

TP: Yes. It is wonderful to see people discovering that.

JK: They suddenly realize that they can finally 'go for it'.

TP: They begin to see that It is in everything. If they are eating a steak, it is still the 'Infinite Expression'.

JK: Yes.

TP: You know, it hasn't got to be watercress. It is such a crazy mind that says, 'If I eat watercress, I will be nearer to God'.

JK: Still people feel it is wrong to eat meat.

TP: Both steak and watercress are the Infinite Expression.

JK: I never wanted to follow the rules as they were presented in religious organizations or spiritual communities. It just didn't feel 'right' to me to exclude one thing and not another, when we are aiming for the *all-encompassing*.

TP: That's right.

JK: But people start to get nervous when someone says that. They say: when there are no rules, what is going to happen with society? What are we going to do? If there isn't any right or wrong, where will that lead us to?

TP: It is a difficult thing for society to accept all this. I know.

JK: Of course, there are certain rules that are necessary for everyday life, like for example knowing to drive the car on the left side in England and on the right side in Belgium. But that is not what we are talking about here. I think it is more about judgement.

TP: And about fear, and about avoidance.

JK: People are afraid that life will become meaningless. Or a total chaos. Or just boring, grey. I don't think that we will suddenly become serial killers because we say that there are no rules in this quest; I don't think our behaviour will change that way when we say there are no rules regarding Liberation. But still people argue that this vision may lead to indifference. That everything will become very 'grey' and that people with such a vision must be very lazy or egocentric.

TP: Yes, they do.

JK: But they don't realize it is not about stopping seeing the difference between black and white; it is just about stopping labelling black as 'bad' and white as 'good'. That's all.

TP: Yes.

JK: I still see the differences between black and white. And enjoy differences.

TP: Of course. So do I.

JK: Another important point I want to mention here is that when you see that there is no right or wrong, you don't have to try and change the world any more. And you don't have to try and change yourself any more. What a relief that is to

discover that you are appropriate just as you are, right now.
Douglas Harding was the first one who made me see that.

TP: Really?

JK: Yes. He said: 'you are not what you look like'. What you
are is this infinite capacity, that immense clarity, which is nearer
to you than your own breath. And you don't have to change
yourself or go anywhere to see it because it is right where you are.

TP: Yes. That's it.

JK: And you made that issue even more clear to me by really
saying again and again, 'This is It', And you said, 'Everything
is appropriate,' and 'You are in the perfect position to see this
Presence'.

TP: Everything is as it is. There is nowhere to go.

JK: Isn't it wonderful to just see that: to realize that – as you
put it – everything is as it is. What a relief, what a joyful discovery to let go that pressure of having to do this or having to
behave like that.

TP: It is amazing. It is staggering.

JK: And it couldn't be more simple.

TP: I know.

JK: Too simple to be true.

TP: A lot of people feel that. A lot of people come to my talks
and just walk out because of that simplicity, because of the
directness of my approach. I know that.

JK: You think it is OK that they walk out?

TP: It is fine. A lot of them are doing that because they are
still avoiding, you see. By believing that it is complicated and
at a distance, they are always avoiding: they don't have to 'dive
in'. They simply don't want to dive in because they are afraid
to disappear.

JK: They prefer to keep on searching. They don't want to
surrender to 'It'. They prefer a difficult technique they have to
practise, they will look for an organization with specific rules.

They prefer to become yoga experts, they would rather become priests or monks, for example.

TP: The mind is so tricky.

JK: The mind is so clever in creating avoidance in every subtle way it can imagine.

TP: I said something similar in one of the meetings, recently here in London. I said, 'Seeking is the greatest avoidance of all.'

JK: It is like someone who says, 'I am on a spiritual quest, I am a seeker,' but I never want to become a finder, so to speak. Because the seeking is so much fun: you meet people with the same aspirations, with the same longings, and you have interesting social contacts, the energy of group meditations, the joy of chanting together, and so on.

TP: I know what you are talking about.

JK: Or you just keep on reading new books about spirituality, you learn a new technique, you go and see a new teacher, and so on. You can keep going on with searching. And most seekers don't realize that there is a lot of avoidance involved in all this searching.

TP: Yes.

JK: I didn't realize it myself until *you* told me, really. But once you see it, it becomes so obvious.

TP: Yes, I know.

JK: And at some point, you see the avoidance and you accept the avoidance itself.

TP: Until you realize there is nobody there to avoid anything.

JK: I think we have been through this subject before, but I just want to make this clear: you say in your discussions that there is no process involved in this, because It is already there. But I feel that − although realizing completely what you mean − there is still some kind of process going on. What I mean is this: there are a lot of belief systems that I have lost since I read your book, and from that perspective, I can see a kind of personal development. It is not a process of learning things, not a process of achieving new skills, but rather a process of undoing things.

TP: Of undressing, if you like. Undressing until you end up with nothing.

JK: A divine striptease.

TP: Yes!

JK: I know it is not a process that brings me to It but more like an evolution that goes with a taking away of concepts and con-ditionings. Of course, it all evaporates as soon as I see that there is no past and no future. Then there is no process of 'melting' any more.

TP: There even isn't a 'present'. There even isn't a 'now'.

JK: Yes.

TP: There even isn't a life. There is nothing; everything that is, is consciousness. And that is what you are.

JK: It is nice to share this, isn't it? I mean, sharing this among friends.

TP: Oh yes.

JK. To conclude this interview, I would like to say that a beautiful aspect of all this is that we can celebrate this 'discovery' among friends. Discovering that there is more to life than just ... I don't know how to put it ... it is just another perspective.

TP: Oh yes.

JK: As you say in the book: it is shared *among friends*. Not some mystic teacher looking down on his students.

TP: I was reading my own book when I was drinking tea in the train coming from Cornwall to London. I didn't look at my book for more than a year, and I thought: what an inter-esting book. [laughter] And I came upon what you just said, 'Exclusivity breeds exclusion, but freedom is shared through friendship.' [*The Open Secret*, p. 8]

The joy of sharing

INTERVIEW WITH MIRA PAGAL, BRUSSELS,
20.4.2000

MP: I am just back in Belgium from a long trip to India and Australia. Very recently, I decided to give no more formal satsang. You know, I don't feel like a teacher, having to explain everything. I prefer to have a relation with someone I know, and then it just happens.

JK: It doesn't have to be organized.

MP: Exactly. And I really don't feel the urge to explain too much ... The only thing I see is that satsang can happen any time, while walking, whenever.

JK: Words and talking are not necessary.

MP: Sometimes, there is something beautiful about just sitting because of the *silence*. A strong silence can be there. That, I still feel as very beautiful, to sit with a few people, and just be, just be in silence. It is very powerful.

JK: Maybe, we just could sit here in silence for a few minutes, right here ...

MP: As you like; I just love it ...

[a few minutes of silence]

JK: It is wonderful to share this silence, isn't it?

MP: It is better than words. I have noticed that the words are meaningless if there is no 'silence' in the background. Otherwise it is just philosophy, it is no more than intellectual ...

JK: ... games of the mind. Endless games.

MP: And real satsang is not like that. For the last two years, I travelled around the world to give formal satsang – which I enjoyed totally – but now this is over. And I knew it wouldn't last. When somebody asked me to give satsang, I just said 'yes' and it was gorgeous because I was carried on a big wave. But I knew it was a wave. And suddenly, in Australia, I saw more and more people coming, getting less personal contact, and I felt, 'This is not my thing'. And I just said, 'Tomorrow, there is no satsang.' And these people didn't realize yet that tomorrow was every day's tomorrow.

JK: I see.

MP: So from that moment, there was no more satsang. And at the same time, satsang is still going on – as I told you. And it is beautiful. But I really don't regret those two years. I met wonderful people, I know what is going on in the world, I know about teachers and so on.

JK: What is satsang, to you?

MP: I think you can say you are in satsang when you can say that you are *just being yourself*. Satsang is just a way to say you live your life for your Self, from your Self. There are no words, of course; you just go back to your Self.

JK: Just saying, 'I am'. Well, not really saying it, just *being* it. Recognizing this Background in whatever we do.

MP: That's it.

JK: It can happen anytime, anywhere. Nothing is excluded: the sound of a car passing by, the sound [we can hear right now] of your washing machine in your kitchen. Tony Parsons would say, 'It is all the infinite expression'.

MP: Absolutely. If you can see that, it is great. When I was with my master [Papaji] in India, I *lived* this with him. He was not famous yet, at that time, and we just lived a simple life.

JK: Seeing the infinite everywhere.

MP: Yes: *everything* was included: making tea, walking by the

Ganges river, and so on. In the most natural way.

JK: Exactly.

MP: Sometimes, people have this gap, you know. They may have glimpses in satsang, but then, afterwards, they have to come back to 'ordinary life' and then …

JK: … they feel frustrated. They think that there is a dilemma.

MP: And that should be removed.

JK: I see.

MP: However, there is no separation.

JK: People are frustrated when they have lost 'It', when they *think* they have lost It. They want to be like their master, they want to become enlightened, they want to be perfect …

MP: Yes!

JK: And when they find out that they still may be angry with their partner, or frustrated by one event or another, they say to themselves that they must not 'be ready' yet. So they say to themselves: I have to do more meditation, I have to become a better yogi, and so on.

MP: [laughing] You touch the point. People still believe in the appearance. I mean, people believe all this because it really *appears* to be like that. Instead of simply getting rid of that 'glue'.

JK: Yes. Why are we so 'glued' to all this?

MP: I think that is the question nobody can really answer. Why do we want to know 'why'? I think that this 'Why?' is not important because we fall back into philosophy, into games of the mind. I had periods in my life, myself, that I really wanted to understand a lot. And that can be appropriate. But that is over now.

JK: All the questions, all the techniques: one day, you leave them behind. Like a stick you use to get up and walk. After a while, when you are walking naturally, you have to throw it away. To me, the end of the trip – if I can call it that – is when all questions are gone. Then you see there never was a trip. I can't say that I have all the answers now, it is more like the end of questioning, of seeking, of longing. It is more like stopping pretending to be somebody who wants to know, somebody who has a spiritual goal.

MP: This is it. The intelligence wants to know, wants to find an answer. When you use your intelligence, you think you will 'get it' one day ... but in fact you will be It when the question disappears.

JK: Exactly.

MP: It's really that. And that is a very simple secret. An open secret [I used that expression before I heard of Tony Parsons' book]. It is a lovely title. I just love his book, I enjoy the way Tony puts things. And he is right: it is a secret, indeed, but at the same time it is available, it is totally open.

JK: It reminds me of the story of someone who wants to hide something very precious, but he doesn't know what to do in order that nobody will find it. You see, the thing he wanted to hide was something extremely valuable. You know where he has hidden it? Well, he has put it everywhere! [laughter] That is the best way to hide 'It': to just have it *everywhere*. The open secret is 'open' because it is too obvious, it is everywhere. That is maybe the reason why nobody seems to find it; in that way, it is a secret.

MP: Most seekers think it is hidden somewhere behind ... that It must be something that is difficult to find. Some state that you have to reach. This idea – this whole concept – is terrible.

JK: It makes the seekers turn around in circles.

MP: But that is the way the mind works. That is why they say it is *beyond* the mind. Although I prefer the word *prior*. Prior to the mind, because the mind can't understand.

JK: Like the face we had before we were born, the 'Original Face' according to Zen.

MP: It is exactly the same. Yes. And in the end, even the mind is included.

JK: It is also part of the game. But I didn't realize this before, this openness and simplicity of 'This'. It was again Tony who made me see that. He was the one who confirmed for me that it is as simple as that. Afterwards, I thought, 'How could it be so simple? So obvious?' It's all so simple and accessible.

MP: You are lucky. But you also have that 'fire'.

JK: Yes ...

MP: You know, for me, you don't have to 'be ready'. There is no such thing as a 'preparation'. But one thing I still believe in is that there is a 'fire'. You need a tremendous fire, a tremendous passion to hear 'It'. That, I still believe in.

JK: I know what you mean.

MP: That's all. All the rest, I don't believe in any more.

JK: Do you think that we may need tools, which we use for a while and then throw away?

MP: You know, I will tell you; where I am, I believe it is so simple that one doesn't need to believe in even a journey. So I don't use any single tool. I know of course that many people did many years of practice, but I don't consider that as ... How can I say this? Well, I will not consider someone's past.

JK: Yes. It doesn't matter.

MP [seriously]: No tools. Just no tools; I don't want *any compromise* here. Totally. Because you see, for example, the great Buddha, he tried everything. When he sat under the tree and he was totally tired of trying, and totally dissatisfied, he just *gave up*. And somehow, he awoke.

JK: He woke up, not because of all his efforts, but just because he realized there was nothing to do. Everything he tried, all these methods, all these efforts, he found out they were useless. He just gave up *completely*, and then 'it' happened.

MP: That is why I am very suspicious when someone presents

himself as 'free' and at the same time presents a tool to 'get' it. It is very suspicious.

JK: Trying to make ourselves better using spiritual tools, is like someone who is looking in the mirror and discovers a spot on his face. Wouldn't it be ridiculous when he decided to try and clean the mirror? [laughter]

MP: Exactly. It is trying to change an image. That is why I sometimes say, 'If you can lose this habit of always trying to objectify yourself, then …' It is like the sixth patriarch of the Chen tradition, who said, 'No dust on the mirror, no mirror.' And that I found 'direct Truth', you see. Because if you still believe you have to clean, it means there is somebody to change. And it is not about that.

JK: It is not about changing our image. I only discovered that for myself when Tony Parsons said that for Liberation to happen, the seeker has to disappear first. He really made me *see* that.

MP: But you're lucky. People always look for experiences, but they forget that the trouble is in the *person* who needs the experiences. They look too far. The first step is just to look and ask, 'Is there anybody?' And then, everything else drops, you know.

JK: Precisely! I love the way you put it.

MP: That is why it is so simple. We don't have to work on anything, on the contrary: we just have to drop this habit.

JK: It seems to be difficult to drop this habit.

MP: It seems. It seems. During satsang, people sometimes asked me, 'Don't you think that this dropping is also an effort?' I said to them, 'It looks like an effort, because you think you were holding on to something.' But it is not an effort.

JK: Instead of an effort, it is more like a coming back to the natural state. It is just a relaxation, a release. But at the same time, people don't want to hear that there is nothing to do. Tony says so all the time.

MP: You know, I don't attract many seekers when I speak like this. Because it is not attractive.

JK: Exactly. It is not attractive to the seeking mind.

M [seriously]: But those who tasted it, know *what a price*. The most valuable thing in life.

JK: Oh, yes.

MP: But not attractive to the mind, I agree. But I told you: I am not going to compromise. I have seen so many teachers who slowly compromise their teaching.

JK: I am very glad to hear you say that; maybe that is one of the reasons why you recently decided to stop giving formal satsang.

MP: What is the point of compromise? To attract who? It is not a help. Of course I have to add here that in the end all is appropriate, everything is perfect. I am just speaking for myself here. You know what I mean.

JK: Yes. We are not judging anyone or anything here. Everybody is free to believe what they want to believe. And we don't need to convince anyone.

MP: To some people it seems to be difficult to see all this. To accept this simplicity.

JK: They think it is only for a few chosen ones.

MP: But when you see 'this', when you really understand how simple and obvious It is, you know that *anyone* can realize Liberation. It is the birthright of everyone. You don't have to be special. This is the beauty of it.

JK: For me, it is such a joy to find someone who has the same ideas about all this. To meet someone who feels the same way as I do. I don't know many.

MP: I believe you, it is rare. You can call it grace, but it is so wonderful *to be just what you are*. When the time has come, that you drop everything, it is … It is beautiful to share this … as you say, it is quite rare, even among so-called teachers, you know.

JK: And in the end, there are no teachers.

MP: No teacher, no student, no teaching. I never felt like being a teacher myself. It is like the satsang: it comes and it goes, just like a wave, but in the end it doesn't matter. I call it a wave, a wave that will not change an iota of 'this empty fullness'.

JK: Yes. What people think about all this doesn't matter any more.

MP: If people like you, good. If people don't like you, also good. It doesn't matter, you know.

JK: That is also a relief.

MP: It is a fantastic freedom.

JK: It seems to me that these days more and more people are 'seeing' this. And it is also more available.

MP: I think you are right. When I was searching thirty years ago, it was less available. It was not easy, I had to go to India and so on. Now there is much more available. If you go to a town like London, there is always something going on. There are so many teachers now, talking about this in so many different ways. There is a beauty in it, but there is also a …

JK: … a shadow side.

M … that is what I wanted to say. The wisdom is totally turned into a banality. And even 'cheap'. So there is always another side of the coin. At my time it was very difficult to find someone talking about all this, that was – if I can put it that way – the dark side; but when I found It, it was very valuable.

JK: Do you think it is important that you talk about that story? I mean, about how you met Papaji, how you found the Truth? I am not so interested to read [or write about] 'personal stories' because people start to compare themselves with the person they are reading about. It is all about 'persons' and not about 'It'.

MP: I don't think it is very important to talk about my own story.

JK: Some people seem to need heroes, or charismatic teachers. And in the end, nothing is wrong with that.

MP: Of course.

JK: There is a lot going on about following spiritual teachers, about achievement of goals, about becoming worthy, about trying to change life into something better, into something more spiritual ...

MP: Yes.

JK: All the books, all the spiritual schools ... Now, I don't care that much any more. It is as it is, and if other people want to search, follow a master, be disciplined ... It's up to them, you see. Who am I to judge them?

MP: Yes, that's true.

JK: I'm still interested in all this, but the interest is not coming from a lack. There is no emptiness inside me that has to be filled up. And as a result, I just see what happens. If I meet somebody interesting, I may be having a look, I may be having a conversation, maybe I won't. It really doesn't matter any more. There is no more desperate seeking.

MP: Don't trouble yourself. Once you saw that it is more simple than simplicity itself, more simple than the mind can conceive, you simply ... well, you just don't want to do anything any more about it.

JK: Exactly. Nowhere to go. Nothing to achieve.

M [passionately]: My God. It is such luck to just realize this!

JK: Anything is appropriate.

MP: Anything. Anything.

JK: You know, I first realized this simplicity when I did an experiment of Douglas Harding's. I thought I knew all about it, but then I really 'saw' it, finally I saw that it was so simple. In fact, I was always looking too far.

MP: But in fact, you already knew it before.

JK: You're right. I already knew it before I did the experiment.

It was a *recognition* from something I knew – if we can use the word 'know' here – from my very early childhood.

MP: You just needed a confirmation.

JK: Yes. And once you recognize It you don't need any experiments any more. In the beginning, It was only there in flashes, for example when doing one of Douglas's experiments. But later on it also came spontaneously, and I didn't need the experiments any more. It happened while I was reading a book by Douglas for example. At the time, I called it the 'rediscovery of my Source of Inner Peace'. Later, it happened while doing nothing in particular, just while sitting still. And then, it became more and more like a background that is coming to the fore. I know that all this sounds like a personal achievement, but it is not like that. And it is not a process in time, either.

MP: I know what you mean.

JK: So It came when I watched television, drove my car, bicycled in the streets of the village where I live, and so on. But I still thought that I should have it *all the time*; I didn't want It to be like a wave coming in and out, because I expected that it should be there all the time. I still believed that I 'lost It' when I was identifying with my personal thoughts or feelings [for example when being ill, feeling upset or in pain]. I still believed one could go in and out. But later I found out it is always available; it was Tony who confirmed for me that this going in and out is also OK! Now I know It is equally available in pain and frustration. It can never leave us because It is what we *are*.

MP: Yes, exactly. It is a relief, to discover that.

JK: But there were still some concepts floating around. For example, I suppose that I was still waiting for some mystical event to happen. I am sure I was not the only one to hope for something special to happen to me. I think it is due to all the stories we read about people who have claimed that they have suddenly attained special states, and so on.

MP: Yes.

JK: Because of all that, I was expecting an event – a transcendental experience – that would take away *all* my personal ambitions. It was Tony who pointed out to me that there is no event to be waiting for. That it also could come gradually [again, while realizing that it is happening *out of time*]. And now I know that waiting for an event is only possible when we believe in time, when we believe in a separate identity. And Liberation is indeed beyond personal achievement, beyond the belief in time. So, finally, I accepted that there are moments of personal identification, and that nothing is wrong with them. Now I really see that these moments are allowed to be there. And that is a tremendous relief. You feel born again.

MP: Even if you feel identified, then what? It is OK, totally OK: you never leave this place! It looks like that sometimes, of course. It *looks* like we lose it, but then, what? Yes: me too, I cannot pretend that I am never identified. And then what? *It doesn't change an iota of what I am.*

JK: It doesn't change the Self. And if the Self is all-encompassing, nobody and nothing can ever be excluded.

M [with passion]: This is it!

JK: And I didn't do anything special. I never felt as if I deserved all this. I did transcendental meditation for a while when I was a medical student, and then continued to read a lot of books about yoga, Eastern philosophy, and so on. I tried sometimes to stop reading about it, you know, but there was what you call this fire, and I just had no choice … I had to go on.

MP: I know.

JK: And I didn't live a disciplined or spiritual life in the traditional sense. I just was very clear about what I wanted and what I didn't want. Then I came upon Zen and Vedanta, and in the end I was left with nothing to do.

MP: As simple as that.

JK: And natural.

MP: And then, you keep *quiet*. When you have found it, you just keep quiet, you are just being yourself. [silence] You know, spontaneous awakening sometimes happens when you get this confirmation. You just need this finger that gives you this confirmation, that says, 'This is It'.

JK: Exactly. It is already there but you cannot believe it.

MP: And for that, some need a guide. And others don't. Because it is our nature. It is already there.

JK: But most people don't really hear it when somebody says that 'this is It'. They want something mystical to happen. They prefer to hear an exciting story.

MP: But what I have also seen is that people don't really value 'This'. For example, in a certain context, they have 'really seen it' but they don't value it. And they go on looking for something else. So I say, one has really to love It and really fall in love with 'That'.

JK: Being in love with the simplicity of what is..

MP: Otherwise you go looking for something else, and you lose it. In this context, I can understand the sentence, 'Don't give pearls to pigs.' You see, you give a pearl and some people don't value it. It is strange but it is sometimes like that, because these people are still attracted by their minds.

JK: I think one of the reasons is that people expect that something very spectacular is going to happen. And that they will become perfect in any sense.

MP: It is a big trouble. That is why a lot of books and teachers are misleading.

JK: I always felt that something was wrong with what they stated in all these books. I don't think Liberation is about perfection.

MP: You know, you have a strong sense of discrimination. Very sharp. It was your tool. You were lucky to have used that tool.

JK: It was my way, I suppose, my way of making the leap. The joke is that I am just realizing that right now, just as you are telling me it right this moment. I was never faithful to anyone, I never was loyal to any system, but there was this 'knowing' that decided what to follow and what not to follow. I can't say that I really decided it personally, it rather happened 'through me'. I looked for a *universal* truth, not some belief system that was limited to a particular school or system.

MP: Yes!

JK: And in the end, there is nothing to discriminate any more, because all is one. And I don't see 'finding this' as an achievement. It is not like a degree or some personal victory, you know. I even don't know how it happened, or why it came. It was 'there' all the time, anyway. I just stopped standing in the way, I suppose. There are no words for it.

MP: And you don't say, 'I realized this because of this or because of that'. There is no secret path. For myself, I also don't know anything about how it all happened. Of course, I met a master, and so on. But in the end, the mind cannot conceive it anyway.

JK: That's true.

MP: The only thing is that it is a great joy to share it. The beauty of sharing with someone who really wants to know, or sharing with someone who already knows, just for the recognition … I just met Douglas Harding, recently. It was such a joy to see him.

JK: I see.

MP: But I was not looking for something. I was not changed by the meeting.

JK: There is no personal investment, no expectations.

MP: But there was the joy of sharing. I also wanted to see Tony for the same reason.

JK: Do you think being who you are can develop in some way

or another? I know that it is 'It' all the time, and for that matter always the same, but I am talking about the way you 'see' it.

MP: I was asking Douglas about this, because he is 91. If we put it into time – I know it is not like that, but let's just speak like that – I think there is a *deepening* with time, I mean, while growing older. I don't mean a deepening in Reality – there is no depth in Reality, of course – but more like a deepening in the mind.

JK: It sounds paradoxical, because Reality has nothing to do with the mind games, with a process.

MP: I know. It is as if you get 'wiser in mind'. It gets vaster. Maybe you can express It better than before. In this way there is a deepening. In fact, Reality is – of course – as It is from the first moment. You know that.

JK: Because it is out of time, anyway. Because it never changes. And still it is never the same. It is full of paradoxes.

MP: Exactly. And we can not go for it and get it.

JK: As we said before: it is the same when we meet. It is not that I am coming here to 'get' something from you, or to get rid of some concept or whatever. It is more the joy of sharing.

MP: Yes. And also, you may get inspired, there may be some aspect that you didn't see before.

JK: Oh yes. Talking about this with people who see this, sharing the beauty of this silence, it is quite inspiring.

MP: For me, too, you know. I also like to meet in this open and natural way. It is not that I am getting anything, I just love to meet and then, this 'inspiration' becomes deeper.

JK: Such a meeting has no goal. And seeing It is about being natural. It has no trajectory. Or a process in time.

MP: And it is not due to practice.

JK: It doesn't come through effort.

MP: This is an important point. Once you realize, then, you don't have to do anything any more. You just see that everything is happening by itself.

JK: Yes. That's Liberation.

MP: When you really get fed up, you are very ready to leave it all behind. *Basta,* enough. But if you don't reach that point, some fascination will pop up. As long as you see yourself as a seeker, it keeps you going. But when your search is ended, it doesn't matter any more, you know. It doesn't trouble you.

JK: Because there is nobody there to trouble.

MP: The identification with the sense of 'I' disappears somehow, so … no problem.

JK: Anything can happen.

MP: Yes. That is what I like about this life; you know what attracts me is to live 'presently'. Then, there is an aliveness which brings all these unexpected things. And life is simple and great. Not great in the sense of peak moments or such, but great by its simplicity. Its freshness. And there is no fear about what is going to happen – there is no time anyway.

JK: You let the so-called future come to you: you don't have to go anywhere, you don't have to reach a particular goal. And then you see that there even is no future. No past, nothing ever happened.

MP: Exactly.

JK: When we talk about living 'presently' we don't refer to 'living in the here and now' from a *personal* perspective [as one can find in many popular books about relaxation, spiritual success and meditation], but we refer here to just being without *any* personal perspective. I mean, not influenced by concepts from the past that influence our future.

MP: Yes.

JK: And when we realize that there is no past and no future, that there even is no personality, then it is seen that there is nothing in particular that has to be done.

MP: Finally! Finally!

JK: As simple as that.

MP: That is the way I like to talk about this, with no mystical or spiritual background, just this simplicity. It is a great blessing. That's what it is.

JK: No religious terms must be understood, no difficult ceremonies must be done, no specific rules have to be followed.

MP: People think you have to pass through the phase of a spiritual quest; I tell you: it is not necessary. It is all about freedom of notion, freedom of concepts of anything. Really. In this way, I understand the word 'freedom'. When you get free from this *burden* of beliefs.

JK: Not just the religious belief systems, but also the inner voice saying to do this, to hope for that, and so on.

MP: It's endless. It's endless.

JK: But then again, people will think that we are becoming indifferent; we can still have thoughts and feelings.

MP: Of course, we are not rocks. You know what I would say? There is no more 'drama' in it. That person who is free — if I can say it that way — is flowing: you don't crystallise things any more. I feel one of the qualities — and I realize that this is a personal way of putting things — is just this: fluidity. Yes: when there is realization, there is fluidity.

JK: These simple words of yours really say it all. At least, if we don't personalize them.

MP: Just being. Not the concept 'being', but just Being.

JK: We shouldn't be speaking about it.

MP: I know ... and still, talking about it this way ... is so wonderful.

JK: There is a recognition going on, a joy of celebrating this wonderful simplicity.

MP: Exactly.

JK: Thank you very much.

Making it clear

JK: When I first realized how simple all this really is, when I recognized the all-encompassing nature of Consciousness, all the questions I used to have disappeared.

NG: You see, this is it: people are going around for years seeking, and in fact, they already know who they really are but they are still waiting for some kind of event.

JK: Yes, exactly.

NG: There is no need for an event. *Right now, this is it.* The final realization is that there is nothing to realize.

JK: But not all seekers want to accept that. Most people are expecting some flash of enlightenment which will completely change their lives. I feel there are a lot of misunderstandings concerning these spiritual events people are waiting for. People expect that they will be in perfect bliss twenty-four hours a day, and so on.

NG: You see, Consciousness – or God, if you like the term – appears here as everything, right now. Consciousness is here talking as Jan and as Nathan, right now through the phone.

JK: And we don't have to run anywhere to try and find this Consciousness.

NG: Exactly. People are looking for relief from their daily problems. Seekers are hoping for spiritual experiences. But who is having all these experiences? *Consciousness* is having them. You see: it's as simple as that. Consciousness appears here as every single person. Including our daily problems of life. This is obvious, really. Isn't it obvious?

JK: I think too obvious, at least for most people. And not

attractive to the mind, as Mira said.

NG: Yes. In fact, seeing this is just a very slight change in perception. This is It, right now. As Tony Parsons says, life carries on as before.

JK: But there is a new perspective.

NG: It is just about noticing what is already the case. And then, suddenly, the search is gone. The search is finished. All you can say is that Jan is Consciousness. *That's all there is.* What else could you be? There is only Consciousness.

JK: Still all that is hard to be expressed through words. Our conversation is still made of a lot of concepts. Even when we say that *everything is Consciousness*, even that statement is a concept.

NG: I know it is impossible to describe 'It', but still we can talk about it.

JK: Well, we are doing it anyway, aren't we? Everything is Consciousness and Consciousness is all there is.

NG: Yes. And we can also say, 'I am That!' Why wouldn't we do that? You are That, I am That! You are Consciousness, you are God. Even without the witnessing, even without the non-doership, It is still there. Even a 'normal' life is still 'It', even anger and problems are included. *The whole thing* is Consciousness.

JK: Those who have read, for example, Ramesh Balsekar [who says that everything is Consciousness, and that we are not the doer], will immediately understand what you mean. But most people … most seekers …

NG: … I think it's the burnt-out seeker who knows what I am talking about. Those who tried *everything* and are ready to give up the search.

JK: I suppose that the burnt-out seekers are the ones who will be ready for your book, for your message. They will also recognize the simplicity and ordinariness of your *non-doer experience* in the garden, as described in your book *Clarity* on page 9. You wrote:

> I was gardening and it was drizzling with rain. I looked up
> and there was a subtle sense of 'me' not being there.

NG: When there was that 'happening' for Nathan working in the garden, immediately I thought, 'Oh, this is It.' What I didn't realize was – like many people who are waiting for an event to happen – that I already knew my real identity. That under-standing was already there. After the event, I 'allowed' the understanding. The event gave me 'permission'. The event became intermittent and then went away and I thought, 'Oh, I had it, but I haven't.' Although all the understanding was still there, I was *confused* by this event, and I was waiting for another event to prove to myself that I was 'enlightened', that I was awake. Then later I read Suzanne Segal's book *Collision with the Infinite*. Someone in the afterword to this book wrote that she was frustrated that the experience had left her at the end of her life. She was frustrated and confused about that!

JK: I see.

NG: It was instantly obvious to me that the same thing had happened to me. I had an experience and I was also confused when it disappeared.

JK: So you had a transcendental event, which *gave you permission* to be 'That'. But when it faded away, you thought, 'Oh, I am not completely awake yet, because this feeling of Oneness is not supposed to go away; this event should be a permanent state for the rest of my life. I should be in bliss all the time.' So although the understanding remained unchanged, you felt disappointed.

NG: But I later realized the event in the garden was just *an event*, just another experience.

JK: Tony said something similar to me last summer. He said,

'You are still waiting for an event to happen. Forget about it. You are avoiding It by waiting for an event, and that expectation will make you believe that you are still not 'there' yet.'

NG: You see, an event is just an event, be it transcendental or not. In the end, it really doesn't matter.

JK: I think that is an interesting point you made, both in the articles in the RMF journal (Ramana Maharshi Foundation, UK) *Self Enquiry* and in your book. It made it more clear to me. That's why I think you chose the right title for your book. And people are recognizing that.

NG: You see, the people I am talking to are those who tried *everything*, they've read everything, they know that *everything is Consciousness*. In fact, many people who come and see me already understand. They already know Who they are. They already realize that all there is, is Consciousness, but they want it *proved* to them.

JK: Yes.

NG: And I am saying to them, 'It will never be proved.' No person is going to prove it to you, no event or experience is going to prove it to you, because you are already 'That' anyway.

JK: It is like water wanting to prove that it is wet.

NG: All this doesn't matter to Consciousness, but to Consciousness appearing as the desperate seeker in the play of life it matters a whole lot, because the seeker wants to get rid of his search. The seeker wants to find, wants to become a finder.

JK: Which is impossible: a seeker can never become a finder.

NG: Indeed. At the moment of finding, you see that there was nothing to find anyway. You were already that which you were looking for.[56]

JK: I think you will agree when I say that a lot of expectations are raised by reading books about Eastern teachers who claim to have attained special states. No matter if it was true for them or not, it is still confusing for the seeker who becomes frustrated at not being like that all the time. Seekers say or think that they also want all that. People feel that there is another possibility and they say to themselves that they also want a continuous state of perfection and bliss. They also want to be enlightened, and they start their search: reading the right books, adapting to the right life style, maybe following a master hoping that It will be transmitted from the master to them by some special event, and so on.

NG: Yes. There is a lot of confusion.

JK: People expect that they will have a perfect life once they have seen It. They expect that all their problems of everyday life will disappear, that they will have no more attachments, no more feelings of fear, and so on. And I see now that it is not about becoming special but just the opposite: it is about the 'Is-ness' of plain ordinary life.

NG: You see, people are looking for experiences, for states. But when they are looking for a special state, they should know that states or conditions – by their very nature – are *changing all the time*. They are looking for something they are not going to 'have'. OK, there may have been people like Ramana Maharshi who lived their lives in a relatively peaceful and serene state, but he still had his problems – digestive problems for example – so he was still an ordinary guy. We are looking for a fantastic once-in-a-lifetime event, but no: there is just *ordinary life*. That is how Consciousness appears, as this ordinary life.

JK: All I can say – for myself – is not that I have attained something 'special' but just that the seeking is over.

NG: All you can say is that Jan's search has stopped, but that doesn't mean that Jan wouldn't mind winning the lottery. The search for awakening is gone. But even when you have recognized your true identity, you may still want peaceful or serene states, and in that case you can go meditate or have a picnic on the hillside.

JK: And you still see these feelings and thoughts coming by, but there is no longer a craving for something more. There is just an ordinary life being lived; nobody else would notice any difference.

NG: But, *you have recognized who you are*. And life is lived from that point of view. But it doesn't mean that you have an experience of non-doership all the time. So there may still be an experience of the small 'I', of the person. But this person has no longer the capacity of searching for Consciousness or God, because you see that *all* is Consciousness. There is nothing else that could exist but Consciousness. And if there is still a person appearing who has the habit of seeking, that is OK. But now you know that everything is Consciousness, everything is you. *There is nothing that is not you.*

JK: And seeing that is a relief. And a release.

NG: It is. And still there is an ordinary life being lived here.

JK: I would say I am still interested in all this because it has always been my favourite subject. But I am not doing so out of a need but rather out of the joy of recognizing a 'common knowing'.

NG: I know exactly what you mean.

JK: There is the joy of sharing this, and there is a 'ripening' in the sense that we see more clearly how simple all this is. So, I still enjoy going to see people to talk about this, or read about this.

NG: When you go to a meeting where they talk about this subject, you are sitting there knowing Who you are now, there is a subtle kind of thrill. You know there is nothing to get. [laughter] There is nothing to get and still you are sitting there and enjoying it! You look around and see people asking questions about it, and at the same time you see how obvious 'This' is.

JK: Yes.

NG: That is why you will still enjoy reading about it, or talking about it. But unfortunately there aren't many people around who are making this clear. There is a lot of confusion. Not all the so-called teachers talk clearly about this subject. Or sometimes people misunderstand what has been said and when for example someone is talking about non-doership, they believe they have to *experience* non-doership all the time. Then comes confusion, because people are not getting what they want. People expect that they have to experience It, but no: all that is necessary is to recognize your real identity, which is Consciousness. And Consciousness is perfect right now.

JK: It is like you said, 'What is right now, is perfection.' But people may misinterpret that. They suppose that all problems will be gone, that life itself will become perfect.

NG: You are consciousness, you are God, what else *could* you be? You are perfection. Yet, you may be having a headache, but still your real identity is known. You may be having pain and take an aspirin, still *you know who you are.* Or you may not take a painkiller, it doesn't matter.

JK: Even then, you recognize your true nature. Despite the pain or whatever problem you want to get rid of, there is *this background of knowing.* You just know that everything is exactly as it should be.

NG: Because everything that happens is an expression of consciousness anyway.

JK: It is a game, a play. We don't have to get ready for This because we are It. We don't have to change ourselves, go into therapy to prepare ourselves. It is only a game, and still it is wonderful. I was talking about this with Mira lately and she said, 'What I like so much about all this, is that now I know that they can never take This away from me. Because This is always there. Even if I tried, I cannot run away from It. There is nothing to give up, there is nothing to get.'

NG: That's right.

JK: And as I said before, I had to wait for Tony's book and your book to see it put with such clarity. But I am sure that if I had read these books five years ago, I would have missed the point. I know it is dangerous to suggest that I was not ready yet, because I doubt if it is a matter of readiness. 'Being ready' sometimes suggests you can prepare for it, that it is something you can get when you work on it. That's not what I am suggesting. But at the same time, there is this recognition now, a recognition that was not there before. And it came through reading about it, and talking about it. Well, at least, that is how it appeared to be in my case, if I can talk about myself like that.

NG: When I am talking about this with people, I just point to the *simplicity* of all this. I say to people, 'You are consciousness, and that's all there is.' And I am addressing those seekers who are really tired of seeking. Who are already seeing this, but just need someone to say it to them. I may not attract many people that way, but it doesn't matter.

JK: And the people you attract are finally also 'You', so why worry about numbers of visitors?

NG: And we reach the point where we see that it really doesn't matter if anyone understands this or recognizes this.

JK: Yes. It doesn't matter at all because there is only One Consciousness, and all those 'different' people are just 'different' waves of that same Ocean.

NG: You see, the seeker is a desperate person, and that is just Consciousness playing the part of the desperate seeker. And then, Consciousness also plays the part of someone who really sees his true identity. That's how it goes. And so it doesn't matter. There is no purpose to it, as I put in my book *Clarity*.

JK: Similar to Tony Parsons, you say that we don't have to improve ourselves. Liberation is not an award for those who behaved well and did their meditation twice a day. There is nothing to get, there is nowhere to go. And you write [*Clarity*, p. 25]:

> The apparent separate individual may concentrate upon self-improvement, spiritual life, or anything else throughout the whole of their life if that is the role being played, but only the clarity of Who or What you really are undermines the search to become awake or to be anything other than what is, right now.

If I had read this a few years ago, I would not have known what you were talking about. So, if people don't 'get the message' you have to accept that.

NG: I noticed, Jan, that while reading your book *Coming Home* you went so to speak through a certain evolution. I know it is not really a personal evolution, but I think your real identity became clear to you while writing the book.[57] You were reading a lot of books [for example by Ramesh Balsekar and Tony Parsons], and you met a lot of people for the interviews, and I think it became more clear to you through this particular way. It was your particular way. That is how Clarity appeared to Jan, isn't it?

JK: I knew Douglas's experiments, and I was familiar with the books of Wolter Keers and Jean Klein, but there were still some misconceptions or expectations that had to be removed. While rewriting the book, there were a few parts where I had to add a footnote to point out that for example in the beginning of the book, I suggest certain things that will later on *appear not to be true*. I didn't do so to mislead people, but I had to go through a certain evolution myself. When I gave the book to Tony to have a look at, about a year ago now, he also pointed out to me that there were some parts that were still suggesting dualism.

NG: I noticed that myself, Jan. For example, when you wrote

that there are three major effects of Coming Home, you say that *we will find inner peace, that our attachments will be released, and that we will be in timeless awareness*. I know now – since I read the last chapter of your book – that you would disagree with yourself, because now you know that these three characteristics of Coming Home are just concepts.

JK: Yes, you are absolutely right. But that part was included in the beginning just to keep the reader going, because it sounds appealing to the beginning seeker.[58] And I also know that in the end the reader will notice that all this is quite relative. Nothing in that book is really absolute; even when pointing to the absolute, it is still using concepts.

NG: I see. I wrote my book *Clarity* in a few days, but you wrote *Coming Home* over two or three years, and it is interesting for the reader to know that. That the 'ripening' came through writing the book.

JK: When rewriting the text, I cancelled a lot that I liked in the beginning, but which later on didn't appear that relevant any more. That is also why I realize that the book – although it was meant for *every* spiritual seeker – will only be valuable to the seekers who have already gone through a few stages, so to speak. I know – again, it is such a misleading concept – that it is not a process or an evolution, but sometimes this is the only way of putting it using words.

NG: I am in the same situation; when I talk to people, the average seeker will not be interested if he or she is coming to solve personal problems like health problems or difficulties in relationships. I am not available to talk about that. For those who want to talk about what the book *Clarity* is all about, I am available. I don't want to make any compromises about this.

JK: When Tony says for example that there is nowhere to go, that all techniques are obsolete, a lot of seekers are not understanding that. They also say that they feel frustrated because they want to do something. Those people would be better off reading a book about Yoga techniques or Tai Chi, or a book by Deepak Chopra, or even learning a meditation technique until they have discovered this 'other dimension'. Then, after a while, when they want to 'know' more about it, they will discover for example Zen or Advaita Vedanta. And slowly they will have to forget about the techniques and states, and leave all the theories and all the exercises behind. It is like driving a car: first you have to learn it, think about it, but afterwards you say, 'It is so easy, it goes automatically.' But that is only true from the point of view of the one who knows.

NG: Yes.

JK: At some point in time, when rereading an earlier version of my book, I thought, 'maybe I have to cancel all the awareness exercises, all the experiments,' because I realized that in the end we don't need any of these. But on the other hand, they have had a value to me, they were – at least temporarily – useful in my so-called quest, and I think they are ingenious. I wanted to show some gratitude to Douglas Harding, too. For his visionary work, you know. That is why I have decided to keep Douglas's experiments in the book. I didn't want to cancel them because I know that they can be a wonderful trigger. So, all the techniques are allowed and may have apparent value, but in the end we have to throw them all away. Not one tool or concept is going to bring us one step closer to Liberation. That's also a message that I tried to put in the book.

NG: You're right. There *appears* to be a certain evolution in the spiritual seeking.

JK: Some people have to look for a door first, and only when they appear to have gone through that door, they will see that there never was any door. That there is no secret path. But I still believe that a lot of seekers first have to 'go away from It' and then *come back* to rediscover It. To *come back Home*, so to speak:

it is like the traveller who has gone to many places, and then finally finds what he was looking for when he comes back to his own house. Finally, he understands that even while travelling he never left his true Home. Most people have to travel a certain distance from themselves [in imagination, of course] to rediscover their true nature. What a joke this is, isn't it?

NG: You have *to have done it* in order to see that it was in the end not necessary. But, even that is only apparent. There appears to be an evolution in the spiritual seeking, that's true. In the end, it is not important anyway. Even someone who never comes to any spiritual seeking is equally Consciousness, is equally God. That is the whole game going on. You see, the spiritual search is only important to the spiritual seeker. For someone who has never heard of spiritual seeking, it doesn't even matter.

JK: Indeed.

NG: I think, Jan, that now you 'have' this Clarity, now when there is this seeing of who you are, it would be possible to rewrite your book completely and just speak from your own clarity. You could just speak from your own vision.

JK: You're right, Nathan, but I still feel that my own 'mistakes' or my own limited visions of what I saw as the Truth, are very recognizable to a lot of seekers. And all the quotes from all these different traditions are just there to confirm what is said. Many readers will recognize let's say parts of their own search, they will indeed realize the illusory aspect of many belief systems. And in the end I have to say that *everything* is illusory. That even the search is an illusory trip. That even the reader is illusory. When the reader really 'sees' that, he or she can throw the book away. Because a book is by its very nature full of concepts. Once you see this, there is no need to confirm yourself by saying 'I am Consciousness', just like the sun doesn't say, 'I am shining'.

NG: It would be interesting to let your readers know that Jan recognized his real identity through writing his book *Coming Home*. I mean, you had to do all the research, read all the books, talk with several people about your book, do the interviews, and that's it. That is how Jan came to his Clarity.

JK: You know, Nathan, the thing is that if I rewrote it, right now, there would not be much left to say. If I wrote the book again – I mean: straight from the Heart – it would be a book with just white pages, because there is nothing to say. [laughter]

NG: That's it. So you'd better leave it as it is, and just let the reader see the apparent evolution you have been through. Reading this from such a point of view may become inspiring for a lot of seekers.

JK: That's a good idea. Well, in fact, we are already doing that right now because this interview will be included as an appendix, at the end of the book. So, I don't have to explain it.

NG: People will love it when they know that Jan recognized his real identity through writing this book.

JK: And I invite the readers to join me in this trip.

NG: Many so-called seekers will be ready for your message, Jan.

JK: And although I do realize that I had to compromise sometimes when writing the book, that's just how this book is. But those who know, don't have to do any experiments any more because they will say, 'It is so obvious, why should I do an awareness exercise to convince myself? Who is there to be convinced?' So, these people will discover the Truth behind the compromises. And these people don't have to read this book, of course.

NG: When reading the proof of your book, I saw you found some inspiration in my first article in the RMF journal *Self Enquiry*. Did that article make a big difference for you?

JK: Yes; it was at a meeting in London with Tony that someone showed it to me. That is how I got to know of you, in fact.

Afterwards, someone faxed me a copy of your article, and I have to admit that it was very clear about what I was dealing with. I mean, at that particular point in time.

NG: You see, Jan was just hanging around waiting for some sort of confirmation or proof. My article says there is no proof.

JK: Yes, that's your particular way of putting it, and some people seem to recognize that. I saw it that way. So, it was indeed a valuable text for me. And I am grateful to you for that. That is why I recommend your book *Clarity* to my readers; but not all of them will get the message, I think.

NG: I know what you mean.

JK: Or maybe they will read the book now, and put it away. They might just pick it up at some later point in time and then suddenly realize, 'Yes, of course …' It is like that for many seekers, although there are others who go a very different way. Without any 'preparation'. If there is no real quest, if there is no seeker, there are no rules, of course.

NG: Some people who come and see me already know that all there is, is Consciousness.

JK: They have already read that in other books that deal with Advaita Vedanta. They just need someone to put the finger on that.

NG: I am just making it *clear*! That's why the book is called *Clarity*.

JK: Why did you start to write it?

NG: It started when a woman said to me that she read my first article every day. She said that reading it over and over again had been so valuable to her, that I started to write my book.

JK: Well, my book 'started' as one page for the internet conference I was on, and then it became an article which was printed in a journal run by Richard Lang [*The Headless Way*], and then it became bigger and bigger. It became ten pages, and then twenty pages, and so on. I took some ideas from here and there, I talked about it with people, and that just went on for a while. And although I didn't want to spend all that time writing, *I just had to do it.* I read interesting books [and used parts of them as quotes, as you noticed], I met new people, did some interviews, and so on.

NG: When is the book going into print then?

JK: Well, you see, it should have been printed last summer, [laughter] but I just had to go on, because new ideas and insights kept on coming ...

NG: You see, Consciousness played the game of Jan writing his book and then having to go through this evolution. It is inspiring for people to see this evolution in the form of a book. It is a unique book.

JK: Thank you.

NG: You really put a lot of work into it.

JK: Well, I had no choice, I suppose. But, I never intended to talk about myself. I never claimed any personal achievements, you know. I don't claim anything right now, either. It is not about me, it is about all of us, you see. That's why the book is written in the 'we' form.

NG: I see.

JK: I don't want to emphasize personal experiences either.

NG: Yes, people hear about others having certain experiences and then they believe they also need to experience them. You see, *Consciousness* is the experiencer. Whether it is doership or non-doership. And this is the actual issue. As soon as you recognize your true identity, you recognize who is having the experiences. Consciousness has the experience of doership and Consciousness has the experience of non-doership and that is why it doesn't matter whether there is doership or non-doership! When you know Who or What you really are it doesn't matter!

JK: I think you are touching a very important issue here, Nathan. You see, today I received *Acceptance of What Is*, a very interesting book by Wayne Liquorman.[59] He has also a clear way of putting things. That's why I will include his book in my recommended literature.

NG: I have seen an advertisement for the book, but I haven't read it yet.

JK: It contains a lot of questions and answers. It is quite similar to what I read in Tony's book and your book. For example, that nobody gets enlightened, that there are no rules, that *there is no enlightened meat* [p. 146]. When I started reading it I agreed with most of it, until I got on to pages 59 and 60. There, he [Wayne Liquorman] talks about having glimpses of It in the beginning of his spiritual search. Wayne talked about these glimpses with Ramesh Balsekar [his teacher] who replied that this was not yet 'It'. I know Ramesh was right about pointing out to Wayne about the *impersonal* aspect of it, and that no-one is going to get enlightened, but there was something that could be misleading to some readers. Before I try to point that out, here is the text I am referring to. Here is what Wayne writes in the book [p. 59]:

> I had tasted 'Oneness,' and I wanted more. I wanted that experience all the time. I didn't want to be hanging around flip-flopping like a fish out of water. I wanted to be 'awake' all the time. The notion and expectation that I could be 'there' all the time, without having the corresponding feeling of being 'not there', was very seductive to me.
>
> Fortunately, I met Ramesh reasonably early on in my search [at least in my conscious search] and he disabused me of the notion that 'I' was going to get enlightenment. He informed me that the experience I had, which was impersonal in nature but was claimed by me as a personal experience, was not enlightenment. And that was a kind of shocker, because that experience of Oneness was

probably the most profound experience that I'd ever had. There was something deeply true about it, and deeply meaningful, because this feeling of unity is the most fulfilling, the deepest, the most completing experience that the body-mind mechanism can have. And what Ramesh finally got through to me was that that experience could be considered to be a taste, a look over the fence, or one of a number of things, but that it wasn't It. He said that the awakening that the sages were talking about was of an entirely different dimension. The Ultimate Awakening was one in which the one who was going to enjoy an experience of awakening was in fact not there, and thus the bliss that was talked about was not a personal bliss. It was the absence – the utter and complete absence – of anyone to be blissful.

(© copyright Advaita Press, 2000)

I agree here that this so-called moment of bliss is an impersonal happening – I am pointing at that subject in my book too – and the interesting part of this is that Wayne says that his *wanting the enlightenment and the bliss started to fade* [ibid, p. 61]. So far, so good. But what I think may become confusing to some readers is that it is said that *the awakening that the sages were talking about was of an entirely different dimension.* This statement may be easily misunderstood by some seekers to mean that *they are not there yet,* that they have not reached the *Ultimate Awakening* yet. That the 'real ones' are having something that the reader hasn't [although that same book says that nobody gets enlightened]. I think the seeker may secretly hope to become like Ramesh one day. That there is indeed another 'higher' state of perma-nent non-doership, a true Oneness with everything, which is the *real* enlightenment. If a reader misinterprets in this way, he is turning around in a circle again, looking for the *real* enlightenment.

NG: Yes. You're absolutely right.

JK: Maybe Wayne or Ramesh didn't want to say so, and I don't want to blame anyone here – but that is how I first understood it when reading it today. And I am sure, Nathan, that you know that this so-called Ultimate Awakening is not limited to the 'real' sages, that it is *not* limited to these impersonal states of non-doership. Even when it is recognized that there is no-one to be blissful! When reading your book, I truly understood that It was there all the time. Clarity is timeless, impersonal and conceptless. It is available in any state, even when we are *not* in an impersonal blissful state. I see that as an important point you made.

NG: Yes, absolutely.

JK: There can easily be a misunderstanding, here. Still, Wayne is right when he says:[60]

> The seeking ends in the dissolution, not only of all of the concepts and the seeking, but with the dissolution of the seeker. And it is, you can say, a merging with the Oneness, a falling away of the sense of twoness. Now, having said all that, none of that is from a personal standpoint. You see, enlightenment is an impersonal event. It is an impersonal Understanding.

So, he really 'understands' what it is all about, but again there is this same danger that the readers may think that they should be in this impersonal and conceptless Oneness all the time. People will think that It is not there when we are identified with our personal qualities.

NG: Consciousness is present through *every* experience. *Consciousness* has the experience, whether that experience is of there not-being a personal entity here, whether it is

Consciousness experiencing through a personal entity.

JK: You mean, it doesn't matter. Consciousness has the experience, and that's it. Consciousness has *all* the experiences.

NG: Exactly. Think of it like that: Consciousness is the experiencer. Who is there? There is only Consciousness. Sometimes, Consciousness is the impersonal experiencer and sometimes the personal experiencer. Even when they are talking about so-called 'glimpses', then I would ask, 'Glimpses of what?'

JK: I see. So, you could say that Wayne and Ramesh are in fact right, that glimpses are only a look over the fence, but you say that there is no need to say that one state is 'better' or 'closer to It' than any other state. In fact, you say that the glimpses are equal to the rest, to anything.

NG: So there is no point in someone saying that 'enlightenment' is a special state or condition. Or that we should have an impersonal state of non-doership. 'Over the fence' is more of the same as what is right here.

JK: If we start looking for the non-doer, we are on the road again.

NG: Consciousness is having the experiences, no matter if they are felt as if they are personal or not. In the end, it doesn't matter. Consciousness is the Experiencer, God is the Experiencer in *every* experience. Whether it is felt as a personal individual as such, or whether there is an experience of no personal individuality, it is still Consciousness being the Experiencer.

JK: Yes, you're right. But most people won't realize the consequences of what you're saying.

NG: The question you should keep in mind is, 'Who is having the experience?' It is about knowing who you really are. You see, from the point of view of the Self, there is nothing that is not 'It'. It is only the little self, that looks at 'glimpses' of anything.

JK: And imagines he or she is doing it.

NG: Yes. Suppose you have a 'Oneness' experience, it would still be known or seen by that same Consciousness. There would be an awareness present; and that is *exactly the same awareness* that is aware as Jan. You see: it is exactly *the same awareness*!

JK: Whatever seems to happen, there would be that same seeing, that same knowing there.

NG: No matter if you have a so-called personal experience of bliss, or a Kundalini type of experience, or an impersonal witnessing of non-doership. It doesn't matter.

JK: I see.

NG: That's why many books about spirituality can be confusing. I know exactly what Wayne is saying in the first text you just quoted, but it can become quite confusing for some people because it will sound to them as if there is something to 'get'.

JK: After reading that part one could say, 'Hey, am I missing something here? Is there something better still waiting around the corner?'

NG: Exactly. You see, sometimes teachers are identifying their own personal condition as *The* condition to be in, to be 'enlightened'.

JK: They are making their own story as the reference. As the final goal.

NG: And there is no goal, Jan, because you already 'have' it. Because you *are* 'It'. Clarity is complete non-identification with any state. It is just being in this state, this moment right now. That's Clarity.

JK: Whether you are high or drunk, it doesn't matter, whether you are identified with your ego or not, it doesn't matter. It – Consciousness – is always there.

NG: Exactly. It is what you are.

JK: And nobody can take It away from us. Even when one is a bit confused for a while when reading that the sages are having the non-doership *all the time*. Even such a statement, even *really believing them*, even *that* can't take It away from us. We can't run away from Consciousness, can we? I think that's the real Understanding.

NG: Exactly. I'm glad you notice all this.

JK: If you really see this, one also realizes it was already there before noticing it.

NG: Yes.

JK: And still, there is a 'process' in realizing all this. And you are a part of that.

NG: I am just making it clear to you.

JK: I think that you have a real talent, a gift, to put this subject so clearly. It is the right moment for me to hear this, and it may be interesting to those readers who are also ready to hear this. It may be a relief for them, too. Or a knowing, a recognition.

NG: Yes. This is the game. And there is only one Player in this game.

JK: Yes: Consciousness.

NG: Also, there is no point to this game.

JK: Yes. First you think you have lost 'Home', and you become a seeker. You feel that something fundamental is missing. You want to find your original state again, and you go around hoping to find it one day. And then, you get glimpses of It and you think, 'This must be it, I will soon get it.' You think you are on your way back home, and then someone says that you are already home. We are already Home! You see, once you have this understanding, nobody can take this away any more.

NG: It is just that last little bit of confusion that has to be removed.

JK: You're right.

NG: There is really nothing to do. But not many people want to hear this approach. This is as far as you can go, Jan. This is the ultimate, so to speak. The game is over, the spell is broken. Remember who you are! There is nothing that is not 'It'.

JK: But not everyone will agree with what we are saying right now.

NG: I know. People want emptiness, or pure awareness. But what is the value of emptiness? What does emptiness mean? Really, what does that mean? Seekers want pure awareness, but there wouldn't be anything to be aware of when there is pure awareness, would there? People want things that they can't get. And that's part of the confusion, you see.

JK: You're right. It is all about concepts.

NG: And life goes on. It's just about remembering who you are.

JK: We can just have an ordinary life now. When we meet, when one day I will come to England to see you, we don't have to talk about this any more: we can just go for a walk, or have a drink in a pub.

NG: Yes. Once there is this understanding, there is nothing left to say. And I am glad if I was a part in that, for you. I am just saying, 'Remember who you are'. I am just making it clear.

JK: I want to thank you for that, Nathan. You are pointing at this subject in a crystal clear way.

NG: Remember, I don't have anything that you don't. I am just an ordinary bloke on the other end of the phone. You are Consciousness, what else could you be?

The cosmic joke

JK: When people ask me why I like your book *Enlightenment For Beginners* [61] so much, I tell them it is because of its simplicity and directness. But in some way, it is hard for me to sum up the message of your book. Could you do that for my readers? In other words: how would you summarize the essence of your message?

CH: This book is a thirty-minute reminder that you already are 'who' [and *what*] you have been looking for. However, you've cleverly disguised this profound Truth behind an elaborately seductive game that you're playing called 'Life'. This book uses very simple words and cartoon drawings to demonstrate, in a playful manner, some of the cosmic [and comic] implications of playing this Game and just how [and why] your Self-deception continues to weave such a magic spell.

JK: What kind of Game are you referring to? How is it created?

CH: The momentum for this cosmic Game is created whenever you pretend that what *isn't*, somehow, is far superior to what *is*. Although this belief keeps you focused on a never-ending journey towards happiness and enlightenment, it also guarantees that you will *never* reach a point of *permanent* satisfaction and peace. Why? Because this whole notion of being on a 'journey-to-fulfilment' is actually the secret method that the desperate ego uses in order to survive in the face of personal annihilation by Consciousness. In other words, as long as the ego stays *more* focused on making the 'journey', it can continue to avoid disappearing entirely in the blinding realization of the *true* identity of the mystic 'traveller'.

JK: Why do people want to change 'what is' into something better? Why are spiritual seekers looking for enlightenment, while you say that everything is already here, right now? Why do we seem to run away from ourselves?

CH: This frenzied activity around pursuing enlightenment helps the ego to maintain a sense of personal doership. When what is *not* present is perceived as better than what *is* present, the precious reality contained in this very moment is inwardly resisted. However, Consciousness has no opposite. It's the *only* thing that's present, and it can *never* really change into 'what isn't'. It just is what it is. By pretending that 'something else is better', however, the ego hopes to survive by enthusiastically pursuing the disowned 'other'. The cosmic joke, of course, is that the ego is caught on a self-generated treadmill because it already 'is' what it is looking for. This valiant struggle to be enlightened secretly protects the ego from being exposed as the phantom it truly is. As long as the search continues unabated, the Searcher is validated as being separate from the very thing that he is searching for. But, in Truth, we can never really run away from ourselves because we already are who we are running from, and we already are where we are running to.

JK: Many seekers secretly hope to become enlightened 'one day'. That is why they stay around a so-called enlightened being, a master, and expect that they have a good chance of 'getting It'. By copying his behaviour or at least doing what he or she tells them to do. Many seekers believe that the state of enlightenment is something that may be passing through from the master to the devotee. And there is also a lot of expectations about enlightenment itself. People hope that being enlightened equals being without problems, without fears. A perfect state, if you like. But you say – and I agree with you Chuck – that this struggle to be enlightened secretly protects the ego from being exposed as the phantom it truly is. Does this mean that all the seeking is pointless, that all the spiritual traditions are useless … a waste of time? How can a phantom ever discover Reality? Is it true then, that there is really nothing we can do?

CH: Gaining enlightenment in the future is a persistent and time-based illusion. It presupposes the absolute reality of a future 'out there' that your personal story can, somehow, live into. However, you are Consciousness Itself, and so you can never separate yourself from the essential Reality of who you already are. That would be as impossible as trying to separate the wetness from the water. Such useless struggling is only further encouraged by the popular belief that, if *only* you follow the 'right' spiritual strategies, you will eventually become enlightened and your personal egoist story will be able to have a happy ending. But enlightenment is not really about seeking something out there. It's only about discovering the essential Truth about what actually *is*. Meanwhile, the illusory melodrama of the world will continue to unfold just exactly [and as convincingly] as it always has. [After all, a mirage of a lake in the desert still looks like a real lake even after you discover that it's only an illusion.] You won't be awakening *from* the dream; you'll only be awakening *to* the dream.[62] But in this awakening, the Dreamer has to eventually disappear entirely. If not, he'll just substitute one fascinating dream called 'Once-I-was-asleep' for another fascinating dream called 'But-now-I-am-awake!' Yes, there is nothing that 'you' can do to speed up the so-called 'process' because you-as-your-story aren't even really here at all. Only Consciousness is truly present, and Its wondrous nature is to pretend that it's not pretending. And so you're seemingly compelled to dance out your part in this Divine play until you awaken to the discovery that there's never been any difference at all between you-as-the-Dancer and you-as-the-Dance.

JK: If Consciousness is all there is, isn't a state of identification with the personality not as valid as a state of bliss or non-doership?

CH: Both of these so-called 'states' are only theoretical concepts. There's absolutely no separate one present who is either in a 'state of identification' or, for that matter, in a 'state of bliss'. Therefore the question of validity is irrelevant since neither of these states are actually 'happening' to anyone or to anything. Consciousness doesn't need to stop 'misidentifying with the personality', and it certainly doesn't need to wake up. It just is what it is.

JK: But still ever more books on the subject appear saying the same thing, saying that we cannot talk about it. In other words, there is a lot of talking and writing going on about non-dualism. What is the use of all these satsangs and of all these books, if Truth is impossible to put into words?

CH: Yes, it's a great paradox, isn't it? The short answer is that there is no real use to any of it. Consciousness, after all, is only seeking Itself. This mysterious conundrum totally boggles the logical mind, however, since Consciousness is already the very same thing that it is pointing to. But even after acknowledging that we can't really talk about 'It' though, we still seem compelled to go ahead and talk about it, anyway. But what's more 'real': a poetic description of Niagara Falls or experiencing the awesome force of the falling water itself?

The problem is, of course, that all words are fundamentally dualistic. When used at this level, the best that they can do is to invite you to look within for yourself. No matter how cleverly they might be put though, they can never logically solve the Great Paradox for you. You just can't get there from here. In fact, there is nothing in your mind that will *ever* become enlightened. Not going to satsangs, not reading books, not meditating every day and not chanting mantras. Absolutely nothing will ever wake up your mind! Why not? Because realization is who you *already* are.

JK: If Liberation is timeless and impersonal, how could there ever be someone who 'sees it' and someone who doesn't'? If there is only One Perceiver ... one Consciousness ... how could one sage or avatar claim to have the best part of it and say that they have come to 'save' the ignorant ones?

CH: There is no *separate* 'one' who either sees or who doesn't see. The play of Consciousness is inclusive enough to seemingly create a universe filled with villains, heroes, sages and avatars. How can one sage claim to have the best part of it and to have come to 'save' the ignorant? Well, beyond this being a classic example of Self-deception, who can really say? After all, not even God can explain God!

JK: Those people who are familiar with Advaita Vedanta say that there is no such thing as time, space and separate persons. And they are right: it is all in our minds. Still the majority of the human population disagrees with that vision. As a result, people say that all of this sounds very nice in theory [that we are not the doer, that everything is just happening, that we are not the body, that there is no free will], but when it comes to putting all this into practice, that is a different story. How do you feel about such comments on Advaita Vedanta, Chuck?

CH: Time, space and the idea of separate persons are not actually in 'our' mind at all. They're only in *your* mind. Like it is with everything else in the manifested universe, the concept of a separate 'human population' also finds its true origin within your own Self-deception. But remember, the Self is only *pretending* that It's not the Self ... and then It pretends that It's *not* pretending. Consciousness, it seems, is a kind of 'experience junkie', and It revels joyously in *lila* ... the Dance-of-the-Divine. In fact, It appears to only remember Its glorious Self-deception with some degree of reluctance. [Nobody, it seems, wants a good story to end.] So if you stand up in the middle of an exciting movie, turn on the lights and start reminding the audience that it's only an illusion, most of the 'others' will tell you to sit down and be quiet! But, as Ramana Maharshi would often say, '*What* others? There is only the Self'. So, how can we ever truly practise being 'who' we already are? Since the Self is the only Reality, It is beyond all effort. Yes, what you say is correct: there is no actual doer; everything just appears to 'happen'; you are not the body; and there is no free will. That's all very true, but so what? To fully dance with [and as] the Cosmic Dancer you are, it still seems important that you honour and acknowledge the appearance of the Great Illusion. After all, It's all just for *you*!

JK: When you say that we are already It, that we are only pretending to be somebody, why do we keep on believing this illusion? You see, people complain that they don't feel like being Consciousness. They complain they are still guided by their personal fears and hopes. They say that life is not that easy.

CH: Well, in Truth, there really is no 'we' or 'they' out there at all. There is only 'It' ... the Pure Consciousness of Self. Asking this seemingly innocent question ['Why do we keep on believing this illusion?'] distracts you from seeing the Truth.

JK: How do you mean?

CH: Well, it makes two basic assumptions: 1] that there really *is* a collective 'we/they' out there and that 2] these 'others' are all believing in some illusion. The question, however, invites you to focus on the 'why-are-they-believing-this' before it's ever been proven that there really *are* any actual 'others' out there to be believing anything at all. You see, if there are no separate 'others' to begin with, then addressing the 'why' part of this question becomes completely irrelevant. Things are just as they are.

JK: Several seekers will also ask you if you aren't simplifying the whole enlightenment issue a little too much.

CH: Consciousness cannot be oversimplified. In fact, It is simplicity, Itself. The indivisible Consciousness can only manifest the illusory world of polarities by *pretending* to be divisible. Amazingly, Its nature is to be what It is ... by pretending to 'become' ... what It's pretending to not be.

JK: So, the whole thing is just a joke?

CH: That's what it is. A comic [and cosmic] game called 'Life'. The Dance-of-the-Divine.

No stone in my shoe

**INTERVIEW WITH WAYNE LIQUORMAN,
AMSTERDAM, 21.07.2000**

JK: One of the qualities of your book, *Acceptance of What Is*, is that you demystify a whole lot about Liberation and enlightenment. And you are going around in the US and Europe talking about 'It'. Why do you do that and what would you say is the message of your talks?

WL: Well, the talking that I do is in direct response to who comes. So, it is the need of the seeker, when he comes, that is addressed in my talks. So I have no agenda, I have nothing to teach.

JK: You just see what comes. You have nothing to sell.

WL: Exactly. People invite me to come to Amsterdam, they pay me a nice hotel room, and I just come.

JK: I see.

WL: The basic teaching, I mean, the way it expresses *through me*, has a lot to do with the fact that I met Ramesh [Balsekar]. I was profoundly affected by Ramesh. So even when we say that the personal details are not particularly pertinent, they are pertinent to the extent that they affect in a tremendous way how the teaching articulates. It articulates through me as a living presence in accordance with the conditioning of this object [pointing at his body]. 'This' has a history, for twenty years it was an alcoholic and a drug addict, and only became a seeker when the addiction suddenly disappeared. And the way the teaching expresses reflects that history.

JK: I think it is wonderful to see – and it is a point I try to make in my book – how different teachers all come to the same No-thing from completely different angles. And as a result, there are no rules. Any way back Home is a good way.

WL: Yes, exactly. The way Ram Tzu[63] puts it:

> You think of the path as a long arduous climb up the mountain
> You can see that there may be many paths
> But you say they all have the same exalted goal
> And Ram Tzu knows this
> There are many paths, like streams
> They flow effortlessly – though not necessarily painlessly
> – down the mountain
> And all disappear into the desert sands below.

JK: So, all paths have the same result – if we can put it that way – or goal or whatever, but their result is their *disappearance* rather than their joining into something. That is why the final step is a desert and not an ocean.

WL: Exactly. In the desert there is a complete disappearance, so that which is seeking, that which is moving, dissipates into … nothing.

JK: A lot of seekers want to know how life changes after the understanding. They are asking this question from a personal point of view, of course, but still …

WL: … Certainly there have been changes since that event happened eleven years ago. Now, tracing a cause-and-effect relationship between the understanding and the changes in the nature of the organism [pointing at his body] gets a little difficult. Generally, the seeker is interested in, 'What is going to happen to me when I get enlightened?' and 'What will I be like then?'

JK: I know what you mean. That's the question behind the question.

WL: It is an *impersonal* event that happens *through you*. And what the effect of that is will be quite variable.

JK: Who would be there to claim enlightenment? Who would be left to say, 'I have found it.' It is impossible to say, isn't it?

WL: It *is* impossible. When someone comes to me, and says, 'I awakened that particular day, and now I am walking around in an awakened state', that is always a giveaway that it has *not* happened. What has happened is an experience, an event, and there is someone left involved in the experience.

JK: How can we still be talking about enlightenment, then?

WL: Well, there *is* an event. There is an event called enlightenment but the result of that event is really of no consequence to the individual because *the individual is no longer there*. So, the problem from the standpoint of the seeker is that it is impossible to conceive of a state in which 'I am not there.'[laughter] So, we can pay lip service to the fact, 'OK, I understand,' but ultimately, whenever the mind thinks about it, it always searches for a 'me'. It's inescapable.

JK: So, it is still difficult to talk about 'It'.

WL: Talk about what?

JK: Talk about enlightenment, consciousness, and so on.

WL: It's impossible to talk about it directly, yes. You can only talk about it *indirectly*.

JK: How do you mean?

WL: Well, by using pointers. And the direction, of course, is … everywhere. [laughing] No matter where you point, it's always there.

JK: Yes.

WL: But as soon as you grasp it as an object, it's *not* 'It'. And that's really what's so funny about it. That is why Ramesh often says, when people leave him after staying with him for a while … He then says, 'Forget about everything you've heard here.' Because to objectify the teaching, to carry it around as some 'thing' is just … more baggage.

JK: It's useless. Concepts of the mind.

WL: Exactly.

JK: Those who are reading about Zen and Advaita Vedanta often conclude that there is no right and wrong. That all the values are 'just in our minds'. Is that also like that for you?

WL: No! Oh no, not at all.

JK: When you watch the nine o'clock news, are you less tempted to say that certain things are bad?

WL: No! The organism that is watching the television programme *has values, has preferences*.

JK: It's not all a grey ...

WL: ... Those who say that 'all is consciousness and it doesn't matter', that's bullshit. That is the state of the seeker who has an advanced knowledge of the subject. He negates all the qualities of things and mixes them together and says, 'It's all consciousness.' When the final understanding happens, all of that stuff falls away. And there simply is a direct response by the organism. And the organism has preferences, and says, 'I like that, and I don't like that.'

JK: Was it the same for Ramesh, when you were with him?

WL: Yes. For example, when Ramesh watched someone talking on the Indian television – for example some politician on the news – he said, 'That guy is a fool, he's such a fool!'

JK: Ramesh still had his preferences and didn't try to hide that.

WL: Of course. There is no bland ... there is still passion for life. There is a response in the body. What is absent is any sense – any sense whatsoever – that what is *happening should be other than it is.*

JK: That's the point.

WL: Yes. That's the way it is. For example, I don't like it, but that's the way it is. That's the basic quality; it is the way it is.

JK: Even when you see someone suffering.

WL: When it is your nature to say so, you will say, 'I don't like that, I'd like to help that person.' Maybe you want to change the situation so that the person is not suffering. Others may say, 'Oh, suffering, that's too bad.'

JK: They just turn their back and walk away.

WL: It just has to do with the nature of that organism.

JK: I see.

WL: But it has nothing to do with the understanding. The understanding only has to do with the notion that this suffering *should not be there*. The suffering *is* there, even as is the impulse to change the state in the next moment, or to do something else.

JK: The difference is subtle …

WL: But it is important. In Zen, the following story is told: Before you start with Zen, you see rivers and mountains as rivers and mountains. When you are more experienced, rivers are no longer rivers and mountains are no longer mountains. You say, everything is consciousness, nothing really matters, it's all one, and so on. And when the final understanding comes, the rivers and mountains become rivers and mountains again. Then, there is a direct response, then there is no filter.

JK: So, you could say that after the understanding, the way you perceive the world is different.

WL: Yes, it is different. The difference is that there is no philosophical involvement now. As a seeker, there was this constant involvement by the seeker in what was happening, measuring it against the principles of the teaching, measuring it against *my understanding*.

JK: That is the state of the seeker. Being involved philosophically. Always comparing 'what you do' with 'what you should be doing'.

WL: That is the inevitable state of the seeker. For example, 'Am I truly looking at this from an enlightened state? Am I looking at it from a point of acceptance? Am I viewing things from a point of understanding? Or am I involved?'

JK: The seeker says, 'I should be in acceptance of what is all the time.'

WL: Exactly. So, after the understanding, all those questions are gone. The experience is like walking around without a stone in your shoe. [laughter] You know, you don't go walking around saying, 'Oh, there is no stone in my shoe,' you *just walk around.* The stone in your shoe is only significant if it is there. You don't think about it, it's not an issue.

JK: That's a nice way of putting it.

WL [smiling]: You just walk around.

JK: Is that the message that you want to share with people?

WL: Well, I don't feel as if I am sharing anything because I don't have anything of value. Some people come and see me, some think it is interesting, others say that I am an asshole, a fool, that I don't know what I am talking about. And it doesn't matter.

JK: In your book[64] you write:

> I had tasted 'Oneness', and I wanted more. I wanted that experience all the time. … And what Ramesh finally got through to me was that that experience could be considered to be a taste, a look over the fence, or one of a number of things, but that it wasn't It. He said that the awakening that the sages were talking about was of an entirely different dimension.

I think it may become confusing to some readers when they read that. Some seekers may conclude that *they are not there yet,* that they have not got the *ultimate awakening* yet. People will now expect 'permanent non-doership'. I think that even doership is equally 'consciousness' than non-doership.

WL: Well … certainly the emphasis of the book and of the teaching is that even the sense of personal doership is part of the functioning of the Self. It is not something that the seeker has created, nor is it something that the seeker will – of his own efforts – destroy. [silence]

Yes, we can say, 'Consciousness is all there is', and if that is understood, nothing more needs to be said. However, if that is *not* the understanding, then there may well be an 'event' in which this misunderstanding falls away. Now, what this event yields, is not someone with the understanding but rather it is *the falling away of the someone* who has a misunderstanding. And what is left is simply *what is*.

JK: Still, some people see this from a personal point of view.

WL: That is inevitable. How someone's interpretation of a certain page turns out, how someone is going to understand this, is beyond my control. It's unavoidable.

JK: That's why you prefer to do the questions and answers, to give people a personal response to their seeking.

WL: Yes. Ramesh could say to some people, 'Do meditation,' and five minutes later he would recommend someone else in the same room to stop all seeking. Or he would say that all techniques are useless anyway.

JK: When you leave Amsterdam in a few days, you go to Germany to see Ramesh. What is it like to see him again. Like a friend?

WL [seriously]: No, it's not like that. It's the *meeting with the Guru*.

JK: I see.

WL: And there is tremendous *resonance* between this organism [pointing at his body] and that one [Ramesh Balsekar]. When the two 'objects' are together, for 'this one' it is pleasure. That is what I mean by the Guru, that *experience of Oneness*. The manifestation of consciousness into phenomenality is the experience of the Guru. That happens when this organism meets that one. There is enormous pleasure for this organism in that interaction. It is wonderful, I enjoy doing it.

JK: Is it the same for Ramesh?

WL: No! No, because I am not – for Ramesh – the object for which the Guru is made manifest. The experience for Ramesh is that he experiences the reflection out of me of 'that'. There is a recognition that 'that' has happened. So, there is a certain pleasure or joy in the proximity of that happening. And really, that is what *satsang* is. It is the proximity to that occurrence. Even if you are not experiencing it directly in the Guru, you can get the reflection from others who may be experiencing that. And so there is an atmosphere of understanding, of totality, of oneness. That's satsang.

For the sage – I make a distinction between the Guru and the sage – the sage is the body–mind mechanism through which the Guru is made manifest to the disciple *in the resonance*. In the *absence* of resonance, the sage is just another organism. If he goes to the checkout of the hotel, nothing happens to the person who is standing there in front of him.

JK: He's just an ordinary guy.

WL: Only when there is resonance, the sage becomes the object through which the Guru is made experiential for the disciple. For the sage, there is no need for that.

JK: I suppose that when you see Ramesh, you are not really 'in constant bliss' all the time.

WL: No. When I am with Ramesh, it's not a constant bliss, it's just a comfortable presence. It's like coming Home. When you come Home, there is a certain ease and comfort you experience. But it's not like going to see the Grand Canyon for the first time.

JK: When you first met Ramesh, it was more like that, I mean, like a peak experience.

WL: When I had my first resonance with Ramesh – it was the second time I saw him – there was a tremendous opening, yes. And it had all the characteristics of a love affair.

JK: Now, it is more matured …

WL: Well, it is no longer an issue whether there is resonance or not.

JK: I see.

WL: There is acceptance, there is complete acceptance now, about that. When it is there, it is there. When it is not there, it's not.

JK: Acceptance of what is.

WL: Yes.

JK: Isn't that Liberation, I mean, accepting what is? As it is. Whatever state you think you are in, whoever you think you are.

WL: Yes, Liberation is always in the moment *the acceptance of what is.* Acceptance of what is *in the moment.* But it gets subtler and subtler. Because 'what is in the moment' may be *dissatisfaction with what has happened.*

JK: That is also in the moment.

WL: Yes.

JK: If you accept that you are not accepting, you are still accepting … [laughter]

WL: Yes. When acceptance comes, that cuts off the involvement.

JK: But you still respond to what happens. For example, when you miss your plane, you are …

WL: [shouting] … pissed off!

JK: Aha.

WL: [looking angry] I shout, 'Goddamn!'

JK: But you accept that you are angry.

WL: Yes.

JK: That's the difference.

WL: Yes.

JK: But when you became a seeker, it was different …

WL: When I became a seeker, if I missed the plane I would also respond by saying or thinking 'Goddamn!' but immediately I would stop that reaction and say to myself *I am not supposed to react like that*; missing the plane is part of a higher plan or something.

JK: A so-called spiritual human being is not supposed to be angry, or show his or her emotions ... the seeker should look peaceful all the time ...

WL: Yes! As a seeker, I would for example say to myself that I have to learn from this experience. [laughter]

JK: The usual New Age stuff. For you, there is no worry anymore about all that.

WL: All that stuff is gone now.

JK: So you're back where you came from. The rivers and mountains are rivers and mountains again.

WL: In the sage, you could say there is *complete involvement* underlying which there is complete acceptance. So for the sage, even when there is anger, even in the frustration, even in the pain, *there is still peace.* The peace underlies all of that phenomenal expression. That is not the case for the involved individual.

JK: But you don't think about that, I suppose.

WL: Again, there is a hidden danger here. It's not the body-mind of the sage that is thinking, 'Oh, there is peace here, even though I am so or so.' It is simply there, and it is not recognized as 'there' because there is no separation at all. It is.

JK: When the understanding occurs, that is what happens.

WL: The stone is not there in that moment, after which there is no awareness that the stone is not there.

We always think that *what is there* is the enlightenment. It's about what is *not* there. What is not there is the involvement. And so what is left is *what is.*

JK: Sounds simple, doesn't it?

WL: It *is* simple.

Perfume of peace

INTERVIEW WITH FRANCIS LUCILLE, EPE
(HOLLAND), 22.07.2000

JK: Each book that I have read, every teacher that I've met, has given me an insight or an understanding which I wanted to share with the readers of my book. I have been putting everything together – like making a new cocktail – and that is how the book came about. But it is not dealing with my personal insights or qualities. It is about the reader, it is about 'all of us'.

I have also been quoting from your book, *Eternity Now*, and this interview is meant to be an illustration of your approach to this same subject. How would you describe the message of the lectures of Francis Lucille? What is it all about?

FL: I would say, 'I don't know', because the message arises when there is a question.

JK: And as a result, the 'message' is different for each person who approaches you. You are not sending a new philosophy into the world, you are just responding to people who come to see you. Is that correct?

FL: Yes, exactly.

JK: And I suppose that there is no personal involvement for you, that there is nothing you want to 'sell'. You don't want to change people.

FL: Absolutely.

JK: Like a mirror reflecting, and It comes out of your mouth and you can't stop it.

FL: Exactly. When someone asks a question, I listen to it in silence, and then the answer just comes. Without any effort. Sometimes I say, 'I am like a bird singing in the tree.' The bird does not mind if the whole world is listening or not. The bird doesn't hope that the listeners like it, but just sings for its own pleasure.

JK: I see.

FL: But the difference is that my song is 'silence' and I am just 'responding' when there is a question.

JK: I think that 'silence' is always the best way to 'talk' about This, because words and concepts can never touch 'This.' They are only pointers.

FL: Exactly.

JK: It's fascinating, isn't it? And there are also a lot of paradoxes, apparent paradoxes. People look for It, only to discover that there is nothing to discover. You know that some teachers say that there is nowhere to go, that there is nothing to discover. You see, that can be a discovery, that there is nothing to discover. That everything is already available right now. On the other hand, some teachers [for example, Jean Klein] are presenting meditation techniques, yoga exercises or whatever.

FL: When you said, 'We look for It, only to discover that there is nothing to discover,' you are right and wrong at the same time. You are right in the sense that there is nothing 'objective' to be found. But that doesn't mean that there is nothing to be discovered. There is something which is at the end of the search, which my teacher Jean Klein would like to call 'the perfume' or 'the sweetness'. The Hindus call it 'Ananda', the peace that comes from our true nature. In the Hindu tradition, our nature has three components: Sat, Chit, Ananda. *Sat* is Being, or Reality and *Chit* is Consciousness; these two components are always present, no matter if you are an ignorant or a sage. Consciousness is always present, Reality is always present. However, the third component, *Ananda*, is not always present. Ananda is the component of Reality which can be veiled through illusion. By the notion that 'I am separate'. By the activities that take birth out of these illusions. So, from this perspective, there is something to be rediscovered: the peace which is inherent to our true nature. When the agitation of our ego ceases.

JK: Some teachers still say that there is nothing we can do.

FL: It is true that there is nothing to do, as long as they don't believe that they are a person. But as long as there is this belief, I think it is better to do something *to get rid of this belief.* Some seekers are willing to believe that there is nothing to do, and take advantage of that concept to continue to live with their personal habits.

JK: You mean that they use it as an excuse to live the life their ego wants to live?

FL: In a way, yes.

JK: Do you suggest that certain behaviour can, so to speak, take us away from the truth?

FL: Well, let me put it this way: certain behaviour comes from the ego, which is a habit. The ego is a habit which has created, which has surrounded itself with all kinds of behaviour.

JK: I see.

FL: There is something else I could add to what you said in the beginning. There is also a joy when reading about this, when talking with friends about this subject. These thoughts about consciousness are of a very 'spacious' kind. And that's because it is the only thought that leads us naturally to its referent. For instance, the thought 'table' doesn't end with a table, the thought 'table' ends with 'Consciousness'. But the thought 'Consciousness' ends with the experience of Consciousness. So any other type of thought is truly intellectual, in the sense that it never gets in touch with its Subject. It is still different from the reality to which it refers.

I remember when I was studying philosophy at school, it was so different from mathematics and chemistry. Philosophy never touched the reality it was referring to. Philosophy was more like 'speculations' because I didn't have the experience of Consciousness at that time. I thought that philosophy was developed by people to waste their time. It seemed to me like a game developed by intellectuals to make money, or to become famous.

But the thought of Consciousness is powerful because it vanishes back into the understanding of what we are. When we let this thought bring us to the experience, and once we have attained access to 'this', we like to go into that 'experience' again. We like to disappear into that experience, we love to merge with the infinite. That's why we like reading books, attending satsang, being in the company of sages, and so on. [long silence]

JK: People sometimes wonder – when you talk about this 'perfume of peace' – if that is really a continuous presence for you. Many seekers have had 'glimpses' of it themselves, and they suppose they have to 'be in peace' all the time. I don't think that you are referring to a peak experience, which has a beginning and an end. I suppose you are rather referring to a background ...

FL: ... Yes. You see, in the beginning, we have moments when we have access to our true nature, we have an understanding. It is a moment in which pure Consciousness is becoming aware of itself. It is a moment which is out of time, out of space; it is very intense. Then, the mind comes back, and has been transformed by this experience – which was beyond the mind. This is the experience of fusion without forms, without manifestation, without appearances of phenomena. And then, we go again and again into this experience. Sometimes, people are so much in love with Advaita that they can go into this through thoughts. Some use tools to go back into this understanding.

But the final goal – well, there is no goal of course – the final state is the natural state. It is a state in which this perfume – the peaceful perfume of this presence – is also present during the presence of objects, during the presence of manifestation. When a thought comes up, it is full of this presence. It is like a fish coming out of the water, and still being wet of the ocean from which it comes. Each thought is still 'wet from its background'.

JK: Yes.

FL: And then, we can have the presence of this Background while we are having a conversation.

JK: I see what you mean. Still, many 'desperate seekers' complain that It [Consciousness, the background] is not there *all the time*. Even when they have heard that It is out of time, even when they understand that we are not the body, that everything is Consciousness ... They know all that, but they think that something is missing.

FL: It has to do with a lack of acceptance of feelings within the body [Francis pointing at his belly at that moment]

JK: How do you mean?

FL: Most seekers can understand – after a while – that they are not a separate entity. People can understand that *intellectually*. And it is indeed possible to understand that – as a person – I don't make any decisions because I don't choose my thoughts. Why is that? Well, if I could choose my thoughts, I would only choose happy thoughts, and gentle thoughts, loving thoughts, or no thoughts at all. So, I don't choose my thoughts, so I don't choose my decisions. Therefore, I am not the doer. All that is relatively easy to understand intellectually.

But what about my feelings on the gut level? When it has

become clear to me intellectually that I am not the doer of my actions, that I am not a person, how does that relate to the screams inside saying, 'Yes, I am separate!' or 'Yes, I am a person!' This almost constant scream of my tensions, of my feelings, is going to generate in my mind a train of thoughts of separation. And I can try to dissolve them on an intellectual level. But as long as the source of these feelings of separation is still alive [again pointing at his belly] these thoughts of separation are coming back again and again. Until that source disappears.

JK: The readers of my book will want to know how it was for you. And if it happened gradually or suddenly.

FL: It is both. There was a moment when there was a 'big shift', but even after this big shift I was many years in the company of my teacher to ... how can I say ... have it stabilized. He introduced me to meditation and techniques on the level of the body to stabilize what I had understood intellectually. To transfer what I had understood intellectually into the level of the body. In the beginning I was still asking questions, but later I was just hanging out with him. In his presence, I was aware of this perfume we were talking about earlier on. I arranged my work in such a way that I could spend several months each year to be in his presence.

JK: You are talking about Jean Klein, I assume.

FL: Yes. I wanted to be with him, because 'this' was the most important issue in my life. So, in the beginning, I had this experience of this 'perfume of peace' when I was in his presence, and then it started to fade when he was not there. And later, It also came back without him being present.

JK: I see.

FL: I am not talking about short moments of understanding or bliss – they were there before I met him – but I am referring to extended periods of silence. And then there was a moment when there was no difference any more.

JK: The sense of peace always being there ...

FL. Yes. Well, I cannot say that I am totally immune to sensations coming up and throwing me out of balance.

JK: Do you feel that there is still a ripening going on?

FL: Oh, yes.

JK: I mean not some kind of development but rather a broadening ...

FL: At some point, problems simply *leave* you, and life becomes more and more miraculous. Life is an adventure that starts like a tragedy, continues as a drama and then becomes an extraordinary comedy. [laughter]

Life becomes more ... like a symphony with an endless crescendo. You see, inside there is this stabilization of this 'perfume', but outside – well you know, Jan, there is no real outside of course – mirrors start dancing with you. Life becomes a miracle as soon as you see that Consciousness is not personal but *universal*. Because you receive such an harmonious resonance from the universe. The universe saying 'Yes!' is a wonderful experience.

Even when you had the most powerful experience of bliss or understanding, you may still wonder if you just made it up in your mind. [laughter] So, you need to *encompass the whole universe* to get the conviction that everything is one single essence.

JK: Would you refer to this as the essence of Advaita?

FL: Yes. However, this insight is not exclusive for Advaita sages: this is the same truth Buddha, Lao Tse, Jesus and Eckhart were talking about. But Advaita may also become too intellectual, too strict. For example, 'What is the use of investigating the body, if the body is an illusion?' That is what I would call 'dogmatic Advaita'. It is true that there is no need to investigate the body *if it is truly your experience that it is an illusion*.

JK: Otherwise, it is just an intellectual game.

FL: But if you feel that your body is solid, that it is not an illusion, you simply have the *concept* that it is an illusion. So you had better investigate this feeling inside of you which says that the body is real ... So, nowadays, we have a lot of 'intellectual Advaita' without true experience of the divine.

JK: So, for you this solidness of the body has disappeared? Suppose you have very severe dental pain, isn't that area of pain, the source of the sensation, extremely real? Isn't there a moment where you would be identified with that pain?

FL: That is true. Yes. But at the same time, there is an absence of personal reaction to it. A lack of mental reaction, if you like. I can imagine that at a certain point of life I could be in a situation of terrible pain. There can be an exceptional level of pain where we are involved personally, yes. But these experiences never last.

JK: And does it really matter? I mean, even being identified, is it a problem?

FL: You're right, it's not a problem.

JK: It is equally Consciousness, isn't it?

FL: Even when we fall back into an old pattern of emotional responding, it is ...

JK: ... like a cloud passing by.

FL: Yes. You see, there is a lot of difference between a sky which is completely grey with no blue holes in it, which is the state of the ignorant, and the sky which is uniformly blue, which is the state of the sage. But when there is one little cloud passing by, it doesn't matter. It is only because we are so 'fundamentalist' that we would not accept such a cloud. Of course, the sky *is* absolutely blue because Consciousness is absolute, but it is the ego who wants the mind to be absolute.

JK: Which is impossible.

FL: Which is impossible. But as a result of this understanding, as a result of the clarification of the mind and the purification of the body, there is this continuous appearance of the perfume of our true nature.

JK: But you still have thoughts coming up, you still have decisions to make. You decided to fly from California to London, and then to Amsterdam, for example.

FL: Of course, personal matters still manifest, but they have lost their credibility. You see, personal thoughts are based on the notion that 'I am a personal entity' and as soon as there is this understanding, you see that 'this thought has nothing to do with me!' Then, we drop it immediately. Jean Klein used to tell this story of a man who was told that his wife was cheating on him. A friend told him that his wife met her secret lover every night at twelve under the tree in the park in front of his house. First, he felt disappointed, then he became extremely jealous and wanted to take revenge. He immediately bought a gun and waited for his wife and her lover the same night in the park with just one thought in his mind, to kill both of them immediately. And when the clock announced twelve o'clock and nobody showed up, he suddenly realized, 'I am not married. I don't have a wife at all.' Then all the emotions, all the actions that have been undertaken, all of that fades away.

It is the same when we were just talking about the arising of a thought relating to a separate entity. Once it is understood that there is no personal entity, all these personal thoughts have nothing to stand on. And what happens is that you 'intercept' these personal thoughts earlier and earlier. Until these thoughts simply stop arising. Feelings may still arise, but we don't let them unfold into thoughts. They are like bubbles in boiling water, they come up and when the source of heat is gone they don't appear any more. Feelings come up but they are not transferred into thoughts because they are just witnessed.

[long silence]

I remember when I was with my teacher, there was this tremendous presence of peace, and it was as if the back of my head opened and that it became like a big space behind me. You know, being a scientist, I had no explanation whatsoever for this phenomenon.

JK: That's the way your organism dealt with it. I suppose it is different for everybody. Everybody has his or her unique path – if I can use the word path. Life is unique for each of us.

FL: It is an endless symphony full of surprises. You don't want to know what is going to happen.

JK: Well, Francis, it was very interesting to talk with you, and I want to thank you for giving me the opportunity to do this interview with you.

FL: I hope your book will be successful.

JK: Thank you.

Embrace life without the mind

INTERVIEW WITH VIJAI SHANKAR, BELGIUM, SUMMER 2000

JK: You used to work in medical science before travelling around the world. I have been told that you had another life before you decided to give people what they want to hear. You give talks to people in Holland, Sweden, Germany, Belgium, and so on. What is your message, if I can put it that way? What is the message of Dr Vijai Shankar when he is talking to people?

VS: You know, you made a mistake. What you just said, those are *your conclusions*. They are entirely yours: *you said it*. I didn't say those things, you *assumed*.

JK: Yes.

VS: Such is life: we assume things in life. Let me make this clear: I have no message to give *to anybody*. Not a single one. You have enough of it already.

JK: I see.

VS: Absolutely no message at all. At all. One day, people think that I am a doctor, that I am a scientist. Other people say so, and so I am what other people think what I am. These days *this* [pointing at his body] is not in the science, it is doing something else now. Nobody is deciding anything. Are you with me so far?

JK [nodding]: Yes.

VS: So, I presume you have to ask me another question.

JK: Well, maybe it is not a matter of asking questions and giving answers. Maybe it's more about sharing something with people ...

VS: Why do you say I am not giving an answer?

JK: Well, maybe it is about something which we share, something which cannot be talked about ... something which is *here* and at the same time has no specific qualities.

VS: Again, those are your conclusions.

JK: I know.

VS: You said it cannot be said in words.

JK: That's why silence may be the best way of expressing it.

VS: No, you are wrong again! Even that silence is a ripple in your mind. *That there should be silence*, that too is a thought. You could get stuck there. One, people understand that the words are nothing. Two, they understand there is no meaning to words. Three, they understand that they have to remain silent. They say, 'I know that I don't know.' And they think they are divine: they're stuck there. It's easy to say, 'I have no thought.' But they have a thought *that they have no thought*. And that is the biggest thought. By saying that, you can only deceive yourself.

JK: So how does it ...

VS: It will be a happening ... and once it has happened, you have landed in silence. Before, you were making *noise*, now you don't make noise. You don't practise it *to not make noise*. It is a happening once in a lifetime.

JK: I see.

VS: All interviews, every autobiography, are nonsense. But that doesn't mean that I am going to sabotage your interview. I go along with you [laughing]. I allow you to speak and I shall speak, too.

JK: It looks like a kind of game: Consciousness talking through you to me and through me to you. Making the illusions look real.

VS: Yes, the illusion happens. You think that you are speaking, that you are a speaker. You know so many things, so many external things. Wanting to know things, there is no limit to it. 'I want to know what is medicine, I want to know what is molecular science, I want to know what is genetics, I want to know what is biology, microbiology.'

JK: It's endless.

VS: Who is the guy who wants to know all these external things? No matter how intelligent they are, look at their lives. They are neurotics. Still the same fear, no love. Still the doubts, no trust. After all that knowledge? You follow what I am saying?

JK: Yes, I am.

VS: It should be reversal. First, get to that state where all the childishness disappears.

JK: Yes.

VS [slowly]: And a childlike innocence comes into you. A child in a grown man. This man values his innocence. First you lose it, then you want it back. Paradise regained.

JK: What do you mean?

VS: By innocence, I mean: not to superimpose language onto life. A child has no language. With language, identification begins, seeing stops. A child sees, but doesn't think. Adults think, but they don't *see*. That's the difference. You don't see things, you *think* you see them. When you *see*, there is no thinking.

JK: Yes.

VS: But it is not a gradual process. Knowledge comes step by step, you gradually grow into it, that's why they call you a graduate. But it doesn't happen like that in your being. [snaps his fingers] It happens like that … snap … You follow?

JK: Yes.

VS: Good. No-mind state is a universe. All the minds … is a multi-verse.

JK: I see.

VS: I only make it clear to those who come and listen. Examine your mind and be very sure what you are carrying in your mind. Has it brought any validity or not? Check it out! When you are very alert and very awake to the moment, you are not bothering about what is gone. And you are not bothering about the moment to come. One must *melt* into the moment, and then that moment becomes eternal. No gap between a moment gone and a moment to come. The apparent past and the apparent future will be *squeezed* in the now. Like a thread going through all the pearls of a necklace. Each bead is a moment. A moment. A moment. A moment. A moment.

JK: Yes.

VS: Everybody thinks. Everybody thinks, 'I am the doer, I am in control.' If everybody were the doer, there would be chaos. International chaos. You see, everybody's life is *one singular event*. It is happening. You follow? To understand that life is just singular, to understand that life is happening, in a passive manner, by *living* it, not thinking about it, you *come Home*. Your real destination is inside you, all the rest is just compartments, like railway stations.

JK: It *looks* like that. It looks like that as long as you live.

VS: Death will take you. [snaps his fingers] Before death comes and gets you, *you* should get death. And realize once and for all that you have never died. Who dies? The body is already dead, it will be the same five elements. Yes or no?

JK: Depends how you look at it.

VS: What do you mean, how you look at it?

JK: It is a thought. People think they are alive because …

VS: Ah! It's a belief. It's a thought. People *believe* they are alive. They are already dead. The body has no sensations at all, doctor. The body is insentient. Absolutely dead. Find out: what is sentient in this insentient body?

JK: Consciousness.

VS: Exactly. Through the mind.

JK: I see.

VS: This body is dead, and Consciousness is dead-less. Who dies?

JK: Nobody dies. Like the sandcastles in the beach, going back to sand.

VS: All are castles in the air. Everything disappears.

JK: All is thought form.

VS: Where is this house when nobody has a single thought about this house?

JK: It evaporates.

VS: It is a thought form. Every object is a thought form. So, too, the body is a thought form.

JK: Mind the mind.

VS: But with what will you mind the mind? With the mind only.

JK: Like a self-hypnosis.

VS: You know where the word 'hypnosis' comes from?

JK: No.

VS: It means 'deep sleep'. Everybody is in deep sleep. Speaking cannot happen in the present. Have you worked that out? Where does it happen?

JK: What I could say is that Consciousness is everywhere. It is here, it is there [pointing at a table beside him], it is everywhere …

VS: No. You didn't work it out. It's not like that. No. That's abstract. That's playing games. [shouting] Bondage!

JK: Yes.

VS [whispering]: It is happening somewhere. Find out where. [shouting]: Be precise! When you say, 'It's all Consciousness', that is rubbish. A tree is a tree, it is not consciousness, it is not aware. It doesn't have a mind. It is just energy, nothing else. You are aware, that is the difference between you and the tree. A bird has no mind, it flies around.

JK: Yes.

VS: Don't think you are getting anything. You are superimposing an illusion. You lose it so that you can regain it again. You follow?

JK: You think you lose it, then you try to get it again, that's the game?

VS: It's not a game, it's a play. A play.

JK: What's the difference?

VS: A play is just a play. When a game comes in, it is about goals, about victory, fruits, money, ambition, competition. A play is love. You play because you want to play. Children play the same game a hundred times. They have *become* play. They are not playing, they *are* play. And they enjoy it. Enjoy the play.

JK: Do you sometimes see 'resonance' happening between your dead body and another dead body?

VS: There are no other bodies, my son. There is no you, there is no 'I' around. There are no demarcation lines. When you have no neighbours, where would you put the fences around your house? You see what I mean? Your boundaries depend upon them. As long as they are there, you are there. You follow? When you are lost, when nobody is there, there is no other person, too.

JK: What do you mean?

VS: Find out. If a man digs a hole in the ground, the water comes by itself. He didn't pull the water out, did he? The water came *by itself*. You make a hole, you make it 'empty', and the water came. You don't need anyone to come and put water into it. People wait for water to be poured into them. They are like a glass that is turned upside down. How can you put water in that? [whispering] Be alert ... Leave the mind alone ... embrace life without the mind ... there is love in the moment ... there is aliveness in the moment ... When you are in the mind, you cannot embrace life, you cannot celebrate life. You follow?

JK: Yes.

VS: Perfect. Good for you.

JK: Thank you.

VS: You're welcome. Thank you for coming, doctor.

JK: You're welcome.

You are the Pure Silence

INTERVIEW WITH MARK MCCLOSKEY BY EMAIL,
AUTUMN 2001

JK: When I discovered your website,[65] I noticed that much of what you are saying there is very related to what I am writing about. At some point you say:

> All the greatest teachers from every tradition have said the same simple things: You are already free. You are already joined with the divine. You are already enlightened. Your very being is spirit itself. You are the way itself. In your realization of your own nothingness, you have realized the nothingness itself. You are the Pure Silence.

It is fascinating to see how people – from completely different angles – come to the same Seeing, isn't it?

MM: There are many words to describe this seeming connection, this resonance or seeing and perhaps fascinating is one of them. Others have called it a mystery, from which 'mysticism' is derived. Still others have labelled this the collective or the synchronicity between we who are called human. The point, at least in my describing of 'It', is that there are a few human beings who in their passionate search for the Truth, for the Infinite, the Ultimate, God, or whatever word is used, have (again through some mystery) found or been found by a glimmer of the Truth itself. This 'revelation' to use an old school word is universal in its essence (There is only Truth) and therefore although the descriptions of it vary (just check out the innumerable paths or ways to 'It') the essence is the same. I think that our life experiences, what we've read, been conditioned to believe or think and probably genetics are the things which cloud the reality itself. So in our meagre attempt to explain what each of us has 'seen' or realized there are common threads, even to the point of using the same words or metaphors. In all of this, the basic notion is the same – the realization that somehow we've recognized Truth itself.

JK: It is amazing to notice how some people suddenly open into this Clarity of what they are. Each story of awakening is unique, and yet – as you say – the final point is the same. We are all unique expressions of this One Consciousness. And what we really are is not that separate person we think we are, but that borderless transparent Awareness which allows us to be what we are. But if someone asked us to describe this Awareness, that is impossible, isn't it? To express this idea of 'One all-encompassing Consciousness', you use the words 'Pure Silence'. Why do you use this description? I know it is difficult to talk about 'It', but still I want to ask you what does 'Pure Silence' mean to you?

MM: Yes, it is both amazing and extremely silly how we wake up from the sleep of belief in a thing called 'me'. The uniqueness is remarkable and the descriptions so varied it makes my head spin. Some are struck by spiritual lightning, some die psychologically, some have a Near-Death-Experience, some find 'It' while in the lowest and most painful point of their life and also many just realize it on a particular breath in a particular moment with a simple laugh of 'oh really, that's it, and it was here all along; oh boy what a dumb ass I've been not to see this.'

For me, it was like this. After a lifetime of searching, it was finally a moment of just realizing this still space within, that contains everything without. A space, a stillness, a silence that is always there, was always there. For many years I was searching for 'it' outside, in a teaching, in a teacher, in a messiah. I was always 'looking' and never finding. But once found, the realization is realized as being choicelessly aware of not only the space but of everything in it. In a sense it has always been there, just overlooked in some kind of Cosmic hide and seek in the mind.

As for why I choose Pure Silence to 'try' to describe the ultimate truth of reality, there are many reasons. As you know there are many names for 'it'. Initially in my own looking for that which is permanent, I came across the following. There is an irrefutable intellectual affirmation that everything is, or has *being*. But for many of us that has become just a given. In a sense we have fallen asleep to this tremendous fact that we are Being itself and the implications of that. So what to 'do' to find this, to wake up to see what Being is? My personal way was to look within myself (My favourite teaching is Jesus's 'the kingdom of heaven is within you') for something permanent, something which never changes, which never has changed. Was there anything? And what I found after going over this large personal list and crossing off one thing after another, including all belief systems, thoughts, past and future (and this took some time) was a simple awareness of the silence in my mind, which was before, during and after everything in my life. And after touching this silent nothingness with conscious attention the result was the response: that I have always known this to be the truth. This has always been in me and in fact ultimately this is who I am, my True Self. From that 'point' I believe expansion begins in an ever widening ripple, so that from the silence or nothingness of this, we come to see everything is contained in this and finally everything *is* this.

Practically speaking I wanted to try to conceptualize and

share this that I 'found' which is beyond concept. I thought of using the word 'God' which is still a good word although there are too many mythic and belief-based connotations to it – too many shades. Then there is the 'Way' or Tao, but I wanted people to avoid any sense of direction or following. I thought of 'awareness and consciousness' which seem to be the current in-vogue expressions of 'it' but 'aware' and 'conscious' are too limited because ultimately silence contains both. And 'it' is also when we are not aware nor conscious of 'it.' True Self is OK, but that implies a 'false' self. Since I had come upon the seeing as silence itself and so as not to condemn 'it' to simple auditory silence, I added the 'pure' part to indicate a silence which is unmoved, unblemished, unattached, absolutely perfect and unmarred by anything we, as forms do or try to undo. Pure Silence is that which even caresses the forms, of silence themselves. But the simple forms of silence – auditory, visual or tactile – are great metaphors of Pure Silence itself.

There is a great tradition in all 'religions' and especially in the mystical or contemplative areas of them which is about getting in touch with silence to find the Divine. Mysticism and all this spiritual stuff was previously set aside for a chosen few, as if silence was not a universal experience of humankind. So I felt that to cut through the mustard of all this, Pure Silence (not merely our awareness of it) was the divine, permanent, com-monality of every human being. This is our common bond. The joy of living occurs in our resonance with silence and the suffering seems to occur in our escape from it – from our noth-ingness or perhaps our refusal to admit our own nothingness. My simple sharing is for all of us to get in touch with that 'inner' pure silence as the no-frills basic step in realizing who we really are.

JK: You told me on the phone that when you read my book, you felt very connected with what I said. Can you go into that?

You also mentioned that there were a few parts – especially about the good and bad balance – where you disagreed. Can you explain what you mean?

MM: The connectivity is so obvious. Glimmers of the truth resonate with the truth itself. There is only one you know. In our personal articulation of it we tend to use adjectives which are culturally conditioned, based on our own life experiences. Despite this, the depth bursts forth. Whether one calls it truth, Pure Silence, True Self, God, whatever. There is only one. I can feel connected to many articulations of it: the resonance based on something much deeper than words or feelings. In my own journey I resonate with J. Krishnamurti, Ramana, Jesus, the Tao, Ken Wilber, the Apophatic Christian Mystics – the Cloud of Unknowing, John of the Cross, the Desert fathers – also Zen, and many others. All of these are 'saying' the same thing given cultural, traditional and historical time differences. I think it's all kind of neat!

As for your own book and my comments on the good vs. the bad, the problem of good and evil, the yin and yang – I don't think I am disagreeing with you, only that, when we try to look into the 'why' about all this we are often left with just the fact of mystery. I am happy to be in a cloud at this point without trying to solve this perennial notion. The good exists, the bad exists; there is an obvious relativity between them which seems to allow a thing called growth to happen. Ultimately though the terms good and bad are just human concepts, which fall away and disappear in the realm of infinity. I prefer to use terms like truth and falsity or reality and illusion: kind of takes the moral dictum out of it.

JK: Good and bad are concepts in our minds, indeed. And so is past and future, and so is evolution and progress. But the human mind doesn't like such ideas. For centuries we have been conditioned to fight what is evil, and human history shows us what all this fighting has led to. Our religious conditioning has a similar flavour. Spiritual leaders often suggest that there is something wrong with us, and that we have to behave differently to get rid of our sins, of our bad karma. Since time immemorial we are driven to work on a better world, to regain paradise. Our ego wants to go somewhere. Some suggest that the final goal is to find enlightenment. We are invited to find the Holy Grail. The person needs a spiritual goal, a target. But what about having no goal, no target, and just being with what is. How would that be? Just letting God's creation be as it is.

After all, the words we use, the theories we invent, it is all a game of the mind, isn't it? Our mind creates ever new philosophies and belief systems, and we all like to believe them because they look so real. But I suppose we are both trying to point at That which is beyond belief or imagination, aren't we? We realize it is impossible to do so, and still there is a finger pointing at the moon, as the Zen teachers say.

MM: Yes, what a seemingly endless game the mind plays. That's why pure silence to me is the final word (or non-word). It's like saying this is the bedrock and no matter what stupid response the ego invents, I can always come back to the rock, or ground zero if you will. I notice in my own life that there are still those moments, though less than in the past, where the imagination comes screaming in with magnificent notions of unreality, always to present a 'somewhere' to run to, to become, to believe in anything but right now, as pain- or sorrow-filled now is. Do you think that this tendency to run is ever finally gone (excepting physical death of course)? Can we ever stop pointing to the moon and realize fully that perhaps we really are the moon? Or is our humanness always to include this limitation?

JK: Are we the moon, are we the pointing finger? Are we both? Who knows? Who wants to know? You see, Mark, it is our mind that wants to know if we can ever stop pointing to the moon. But the danger is that our mind turns all this into a new concept. A new understanding which has to be remembered. And we are not talking here about some new 'theory' or a new belief system.

To make this clear, we have to start from the very basic questions; 'Who or what am I?', 'Is somebody there?', 'Is there any goal to attain?'. When I ask you to write down your life story on a paper, you can write down your name, your day of birth, where you grew up. You explain what you do in life, you may even make a drawing of how you look or add a photograph. That is your image of yourself. You also add a list of your main characteristics: your qualities, your skills, how people say you are, and so on. Now the question is, 'Is that image really you?'. Are you that picture, those words and concepts, or do you feel inside that you are much more than that? I am sure you just know that you are so much more than that person you described. So much more than that body and mind, sitting here reading this text. To use the same metaphor, you see that what you really are is not just an image of a person but also the white paper you are writing your story on. You are both, depending on your point of view. The 'human part' and the 'Being part'. The human part being the limited person you think you are, and the Being part the unlimited consciousness in which your life story appears.

So, there seem to be two ways of looking at this. If you just notice the person as described above, that is what you think you are and that is OK. It is the little guy in the mirror in the bathroom every morning. You limit yourself to the person on your passport. The one who wants to run from here to there. The man with a past and a future. However, when you put on a wide-angle lens you see the greater picture. It may dawn on you during a transcendental event or while walking in a forest, but suddenly you see that everything is connected, and that 'you' are not separate from 'It'. You see you are both the cloud and the sky, both the wave and the ocean. You discover your 'Being part' which includes your human part.

On the other hand, you are right in saying that our humanness always includes some limitation. The 'human part' has its limits: that is inevitable. And there is nothing wrong with identifying ourselves with the person we think we are – for practical reasons. In fact, it is impossible to escape from the prison we created for ourselves, as long as this body is alive. From the point of view of the limited person – what I call vision X in the book *Nobody Home* – there is no escape from our daydream. But vision Y – the vision I point to in my book as the 'greater' vision – is not ignoring the limits of vision X, but is just a broader approach. It includes vision X.[66] It includes the Light and the white canvas on which our (personal) movie is projected. Even when you have fears or plans or hopes, even then your true nature is the Ocean. Seeing that may be very liberating. But not seeing that is also OK. Nothing can be excluded.

In the beginning, it may look as if we are switching over from vision X to vision Y, but after a while we see that all is One. And finally we understand that we *are* the light. Suddenly it is clear: we are the Light that shines in our movie, and that shines in or through all the other movies. And that is what connects us all; a unique all-encompassing Consciousness. And as we have no words for it, it is better to be silent about This. That is why – again – I like your description 'Pure Silence'.

MM: Obviously I resonate and concur with what you are saying. There is no denying the fact that we have a brain which has been conditioned to believe itself to be the 'source' and 'centre' of everything and wants and needs to know more and more. The whole purpose of transformative practice is to either suddenly or gradually unhook from the separate X-vision and realize that we are merely awash in the pure silent void which is the unifying ground of One. Physiologically speaking we must come to realize that our brain is 'plugged-in' to this thing called silence, Consciousness, God, whatever – not that our individual mind is the controller itself. And more than that: our bodies and brains are found within silence or consciousness itself – not the other way around.

But tell me Jan, it is one thing to talk of all this and make a declaration to the world that you and I see this and that the movie exists. It is quite another to integrate this vision into living. After all what good is any 'spirituality' if humanity does not embrace it – in other words lives daily out of pure silence or out of the Self, or from the place called 'Home'. It seems to me that seeing the True Self as it is, implies that life becomes 'selfless service' to that truth and each of us has an implicit duty to shine to all those still in illusion. I find that most authors writing about the Spirit leave it there as some disembodied entity. To me that is not what it's about. Ultimately we have responsibility to be compassion itself. The only thing we can do is plunge into the flesh, into suffering, and perhaps try to enlighten the dark parts of the movie. I don't remember who said it but there is an adage 'Enlightenment is not personal, it's for the whole, the other, as well'. I'm interested in your thoughts on this as well.

JK: I am not sure whether we have to integrate our vision into living. I wonder what is the real reason for saving the world. And according to what standards are we going to do that? We all know what the results are if two groups want to destroy the evil in the world, when both of them have opposite opinions on what is good and what is bad. I really wonder if all this struggle against 'evil' is really doing humanity any good.

I wonder why we have to try to enlighten the dark parts of

the movie. *Can* we do so, or do we *think* we can? As the world is right now, that is 'It'. My (or your) personal opinion on what is happening in the world is just another cloud passing by. And all those clouds are also 'It'. And if you or someone else feels like spreading spirituality, that is also 'It'. I can't criticize that. And if you think that we have an implicit duty to shine to all those still in illusion, that is also 'It'. But those people in illusion are also 'It' and they are not one inch further away from 'It' than we are. I don't see any boundaries any more. How would I dare to create any separation? I have no tools any more to judge anyone or anything. How could I criticize God's creation? All I am left with is this 'pure silence' which leaves me with no tools for judgment or criticism. And that may sound threatening to many, but for me it is total freedom. Not freedom for Jan, but just naked freedom in itself. As such, enlightenment is not personal, it is for the whole indeed. This 'coming Home' is for all the others as well – because there are no 'others'. That is why my second book is called *Nobody Home*: the separation is an illusion, and so are all the theories based on individuality.

I realize that some words of mine may sound as if I am sitting behind a wall of glass, looking at the world from a distance. That I don't care any more about the suffering of my fellow people. Let me tell you that it is just the opposite. When separation is seen as illusory, it doesn't mean that the other person's ego is illusory; it also means that my ego is illusory. And that I am not separate from them. In that Oneness, there are no rules to take care of your neighbour as for yourself, because there is no more separation! Any sense of separation is only a mental image in our minds. And knowing that does not prevent you from helping your neighbour. Helping those in need just happens spontaneously.

Seeing that there is nobody home, that there is only One,

may open us up to whatever is appearing, without any personal agenda. It may reveal the source of unconditional love, of true compassion, quite naturally, not because we feel as if we have to save the world. Then there is only Silence and in that silence the apparent world appears as a magic snapshot. Like those words from you on your website:

> There is a gentle, loving, peace-filled silence here and now in this moment. It has always been this way. It is always here. It is right here within you and all around you, a stillness, an apparent void, a seeming nothingness out of which everything arises, exists, and eventually returns. You know this. You have felt this. There is nothing more than this. You are this.

The place of not-knowing

INTERVIEW WITH ECKHART TOLLE,
HOLLAND, 17.04.02

JK: The story which you describe in the introduction to your book[67] is that for many years you lived in a state of fear and depression. And that it became so unbearable that suddenly the thought occurred to you, 'I cannot live with myself any longer.'

ET: That thought was like a Zen koan: it destroyed conceptual thinking. That particular thought was the trigger for a deep transformation because I wondered, 'Who is the 'I' and who is the self that I cannot live with?' At that moment the identification with the 'unhappy me' disappeared completely. The next morning, I was walking around in stillness.

JK: I see.

ET: I knew there was deep peace, and the activity of the mind was reduced by eighty to ninety percent. That went on with great intensity for several months. It never left me, but the intensity varies. Sometimes the stillness is in the background, sometimes it fills everything, but it is always there.

JK: The story goes that you spent two years living on park benches before you started to talk about this.

ET: I was lost in Being. The present moment was so fulfilling that I had completely lost interest in the future. The future and all the rest didn't matter any more. I was in some sort of continuous state of joy. Sometimes my mind would come in and ask, 'How can you be so happy?'

JK: You got lost in Beingness?

ET: Yes. One aspect of the transformation that happened to me was that the stream of thinking became reduced considerably.

JK: You were walking around with very little thought?

ET: Yes. I was walking around with very little thought. Without realizing it.

JK: I see.

ET: The wonderful thing is to relate to the world and yourself without the screen of interpretation and conceptualization. So, not relating to yourself and others through mental noise but through stillness.

JK: That is what awakening means to you?

ET: Yes: knowing yourself to be the stillness.

JK: At that time, you were so to speak lost in this stillness.

ET: But gradually I managed to function in that new state so that I could function in the world again. I couldn't be sitting on a park bench in Russell Square for the rest of my life. I gradually regained the balance between being and doing.

JK: And finally some people had recognized some sort of transformation in you. That is how your teaching started, isn't it?

ET: Yes, it started gradually.

JK: When that joy appeared, did you realize what exactly happened to you?

ET: No. You see, I didn't have any spiritual teachers at that time, and I had no understanding of what happened to me.

JK: So you had the sense of peace without understanding it. Is that when you started to read about the subject?

ET: Yes, I started reading books about the subject, and also visiting teachers. And in many cases there was a deep recognition. I resonated with what some Buddhist teachers said, and also with the Bhagavad Gita and the Tao Te Ching.

JK: So you started reading all this *after* 'your' awakening?

ET: Yes, indeed. I only had a brief look at a Krishnamurti

book, although I didn't understand it at the time. I also tried philosophy, but I soon realized that the academic world didn't have the answers I was looking for.

JK: When people ask you about your personal life, and how the transformation happened to you, there is this danger we may get stuck in the personal instead of the impersonal.

ET: Yes.

JK: The presence you talked about today has nothing to do with our personal life, does it? And 'It' is here, right now. All these 'stories' are personalized, and that is not really important.

ET: No, it is not relevant.

JK: Still there is one point I want to ask you about. People seem to report that being in your neighbourhood seems to give them the opportunity to recognize this presence.

ET: Yes.

JK: Normally, in daily life, they don't recognize 'It'. Can you explain what is happening? And why those people don't recognize this in their daily life, while they do when they are listening to you?

ET: That is always part of any true spiritual teaching, that the words that come out are only one aspect of the teaching – but not even the most important aspect of the teaching. Although I avoid using any esoteric language, I could say that this state is transmitting itself. It can happen while the words are spoken, but it can also happen through silence. In silence. There are even other forms of transmission, like sound, touch.

JK: Yes.

ET: It seems to happen that it is also transmitted through the written word. It is flowing out of that state. It is in the book *The Power of Now* which people have read many times, and every time the energy is fresh and new. Any spiritual writing that comes out of this presence also contains that energy field. So, the presence of the teacher may even be stronger than the writing. The power of spiritual discourse – whether it is written or spoken – is that there is more than just the words. One could say that those words go deeper into the listener than words that are purely informational. When the words are purely informational, they are decoded by the mind and that's it.

JK: Then it is just an intellectual process.

ET: Yes. But here they are also decoded by the mind and then they continue – the energy of it continues to go deeper …

JK: It echoes … it resonates …

ET: Yes. And then it awakens presence in the listener – or the reader. It awakens – or one could say – it almost pours it out. It works on a deeper level. One could say that presence recognizes itself.

JK: Like a mirror.

ET: Yes.

JK: In fact, there is only one presence, which is reflected in many forms, including your book.

ET: Yes.

JK: What I found amazing is to discover that the person we all think is inside, is simply not there. That there is in fact no person living inside.

ET: Yes.

JK: Of course, it is not very popular to say so, your audience might say, 'Oh, this is becoming too much,' or 'This is strange.'

ET: Yes.

JK: But in a way it is true.

ET: Oh yes.

JK: The idea of a person who is living inside our body is just a cloud passing by.

ET: Yes, that's right.

JK: And today you talked a lot about the 'pain body'. That what you describe as the human suffering we carry with us. In a way, one could say that the idea of a pain body living inside our body is also just a cloud passing by.

ET: Yes, that's right. Or a dream.

JK: And so is time.

ET: The amazing thing about 'time' is that we need it for everything in life, except for the most vital thing there is, which is knowing yourself at the deepest level. Not only do you not need time, but the concept of time is the greatest obstacle to that.

JK: How do you deal with the pain body that was connected to you, to Eckhart before he became what he is right now? If something comes up now, is it like a witnessing? How would you describe it?

ET: I sometimes feel the human pain body ... well, the personal flavour is gone ... I sometimes feel the human pain body ... and I immediately recognize that as non-personal. [silence] [seriously] But sometimes I cry. Sometimes I cry when I ... what are they doing to themselves? You see?

JK: But you recognize those mechanisms now ...

ET: Yes.

JK: It is mirrored in your own body and you sense that.

ET: And when it is totally accepted – even these human pains – the tears ... the pain ... it turns around. [smiling] On the other side of the pain there is the joy.

JK: Yes! Black and white, always in the divine balance.

ET: Oh yes.

JK: It is interesting to see that these days, spiritual teachers – if I can use that word – are taking distance from the old religious dogmas.

ET: Yes.

JK: I sense that more and more teachers dare to say that there are no rules. That you don't have to behave in a certain way.

ET: Yes.

JK: It is sometimes said that there is a new consciousness growing, which allows it to really say so. A few centuries ago, they would burn you to death to say such things in public. You would be a danger in the eyes of the religious organizations.

ET: Yes.

JK: We seem to live in a unique situation, where teachers are now allowed to say all this.

ET: Oh yes.

JK: Teachers are allowed to say how simple it all is.

ET: Yes. That is how it is going these days.

JK: Everybody is invited to come home to what is.

ET: Yes.

JK: Until we realize that in fact there is nobody to finally get 'It'. The person who wants to come Home is standing in the way, in fact.

ET: Oh yes.

JK: And people are now recognizing the simplicity of this message. They just go 'Oh!'.

ET: Yes.

JK: A lot of people sensed this during your talk today.

ET: Oh, yes.

JK: They see the mechanisms of their minds, and suddenly sense that 'It' is here.

ET: Yes. In silence, or by just being there.

JK: Even right now, while we are sitting here talking, it is fully available.

ET: Yes.

JK: It doesn't need talking about.

ET: Not at all.

JK: Just sharing this – without trying to prove something or trying to get something.

ET: Yes. It is very accessible now.

JK: Yes.

ET: Before, it was exclusive. And people identified it with the 'form' through which it came ... the structure of the religion, the mind structure that went with it.

JK: Yes.

ET: So, there is a freedom now, so that it does not get mixed up with forms. That's the beauty of it.

JK: Do you feel for yourself that you have a particular task in this new consciousness?

ET: Yes.

JK: How do you feel about it? Your books are worldwide best-sellers now, translated in many languages. You go around talking about it. People want to come and see you, they really want to hear you. Is there something you have to add into this?

ET: Yes. I sense the opening for that. And I am just available for that.

JK: Yes.

ET: I am not doing it at all. There is a beautiful little poem that says, 'I am a hole in the flute that the priceless walks through. Listen to this music.'

JK: So, you can't help it.

ET: Yes.

JK: Would you agree if I said that the Eckhart – the person Eckhart Tolle – is not involved in all this.

ET: Yes.

JK: Is it like you watch words coming out of your mouth?

ET: Yes.

JK: Without making this mystical or special. The person who thinks he is important would only be standing in the way.

ET: Yes.

JK: It is like suddenly realizing, 'Is it as simple as that?'.

ET [laughing]: Yes.

JK: How can we tell people that it is more simple than the mind ever can imagine? The mind wants to make it special, project it into the future, and it is here ...

ET [laughing]: Yes. That's right.

JK: There is joy in this sharing, isn't there?

ET: Yes.

JK: But this isn't the joy of the mind I am referring to.

ET: No.

JK: This is the joy of the background. This is not a joy you can get used to. Everything is included. Nothing can be excluded.

ET: No.

JK: There is only alignment with the 'now' as you called it today.

ET: Yes. Oh, yes.

JK: Even pain. Even pain and suffering can't be excluded. It is all the divine balance.

ET: It is in the 'yes to the now' that nothing is excluded. Everything is embraced.

JK: Yes.

ET: And I see it accelerating in time, if I can say that, accelerate on the planet.

JK: We could even say that if some people don't see this, it doesn't matter either.

ET: No. That's right.

JK: When you see it is everywhere, it is not necessary to convince people of this, because it doesn't matter anyway. Even pain and problems are an expression of it. Even the pain body is an invitation to see this.

ET: When you are identified with that, then it's a dream. And then 'it' is there, too [laughing].

JK: What is it like for you to travel around and talk about your book *The Power of Now*?

ET: It is like a responding to a demand, to an invitation. There is an invitation, and there is a response.

JK: It is like it is all happening beyond your own will or your own ideas. It is just happening, isn't it?

ET: Yes. Oh yes, completely.

JK: You can't help it. It just happens, so to speak.

ET: Yes.

JK: As we said earlier, the 'old' Eckhart, the character you used to be before, is not involved in this.

ET: No.

JK: And at the same time, you still behave like a 'normal' person. I mean, you don't behave like a special person, like a guru or saint. I think it is an important quality of today's spiritual teachers so to speak, that many of them – not all of them – are not trying to be special.

ET: Yes. This has nothing to do with specialness.

JK: And specialness creates distance.

ET: Yes. Particularly teachers who are surrounded exclusively by disciples – for example in an ashram – they never meet anyone out there who is not a devotee. And then, after a few years of this projection of specialness, it is possible – I have seen it happen – for the delusion to return.

JK: They imagine they are special, that they have to save the world, and so on.

ET: Yes.

JK: They imagine they are sent by God personally to do this and to do that.

ET: Yes.

JK: It is all division.

ET: Yes.

JK: Division between a teacher who is special and his devotees who are ordinary.

ET: Yes. It is all very seductive to the ego. And to the egos surrounding the teachers. That is how cults and sects appear. All of them are expressions of the egoic consciousness.

JK: These teachers point to what is different between you and me. In my book, I try to point to that which is the same between you and me and everyone else. For example, when I look at you, I see two eyes over there, and I don't see any eyes here, but only aware consciousness.

ET: Yes.

JK: And this is the same for you. We all share this one consciousness.

ET [laughing]: Yes.

JK: Like this octopus with six billion arms: many different manifestations, and still one consciousness.

ET: Yes, but then the mind comes in and interprets it, and reinterprets it. And what is one then becomes divided. Religion – although the core of it is usually very true – divides what is one.

JK: Yes.

ET: Religions tend to become divided because they are mind creations. Although when you look deep enough, there is the core, there is still the true silence, behind the heavy layers of time and thinking.

JK: Today you talked about the alignment with 'now'. When this is a reality, when one doesn't say 'no' any more to what is, you are expected to behave in a certain way. People expect that their life will be changed in a certain way. They hope that seeing this will make their life perfect. But I feel that you will agree that nothing really changes, but that the personal investment, the personal involvement disappears.

ET: Yes. Life tends to flow with greater ease. There are more harmonious interactions with other humans. The harmony comes into that. Nevertheless you do still face the limitations of form. All kind of situations. Things can go wrong. Forms may limit you. That remains.

JK: Could you say you may still appear the 'old Eckhart' so to speak? After all what happened? Can you still be the old one, without being involved?

ET: Yes, yes. Certain behaviour patterns that are part of the form, they remain.

JK: There is nothing wrong with that.

ET. No. It may be the way someone walks, for example.

JK: Yes.

ET: The teaching flows through a certain form, and it really doesn't matter. It may even vary depending on the astrological sign of the teacher.

JK: Mm. The colours of the teaching may vary, but the Beingness the teaching points to is always the same.

ET: Yes.

JK: And people seem to understand now that this is not related to a specific behaviour.

ET: No.

JK: So there is nothing to exclude.

ET: That's right.

JK: And I think more and more people are sensing that.

ET: Yes.

JK: As soon as you say to someone, 'Don't do that' you are already dividing things. As soon as you are saying, 'This is not good', you are dualistic.

ET: Yes.

JK: Isn't it a joy for you to be able to share this with so many people?

ET: Yes, absolutely. I talk almost every other day, travelling from one city to another. There is a joy in sharing this, and although one could say that I always talk about more or less the same thing, it feels fresh and new every time. As I said earlier today in the talk, it is always new [laughing].

JK: You always start from zero.

ET: Yes.

JK: And you can't help it.

ET: Yes, that's right. It all comes from the place of not-knowing.

Revelation of
the divine hand

JK: What is it like for you to travel around the world talking about 'The Absolute'?

FL: I enjoy doing it. And I just do it. I enjoy meeting truth-lovers, truth-seekers.

JK: It must be quite a different life compared with the one you had in France before you came into all this, before you met your teacher Jean Klein.

FL: Oh, all this is a very long time ago. I met this perspective when I was about thirty years old, and now I am fifty-seven.

JK: When I looked at the flyer which describes your satsangs, I noticed a kind of ripening in the way you express what you call Consciousness. I know that what you are referring to is always the same, but maybe you are more alive and fresh about It than a few years ago.

FL: Yes, the expression changes, but I can't say it is better. I still agree with what I said ten years ago.

JK: Your website states you talk about one thing: *awareness, our true nature, the Absolute*. In some way, it must be difficult to talk about that which is always available, while not trying to be special or holy. You know that a lot of spiritual teachers are behaving in a special or so-called holy way. Sometimes this behaviour is inspired by the Eastern traditions.

FL: The truth is not from the East or from the West. The

teacher of my teacher was from Bangalore and he was not behaving like a holy man, but rather was a 'normal' man. And if someone took him for a guru, he would take anyone for a guru because there is only one guru.

JK: Still a lot of people like to project the infinity into a holy person or into some state in the future. But I would say that the Absolute cannot be projected into a future state. Nor that 'It' can be achieved by following certain rules. Would you agree that indeed there is no path, that there is no way to behave?

FL: Yes. But what matters is not what is said but where the words come from. Someone can take the words of the teaching without having the understanding and the experience. It is the inner experience where the words come from which counts. So, the words in a way can contradict each other, but what counts is where the words come from.

JK: I see.

FL: It is an art form, in a way. True art comes from presence and points to presence. And what is said during satsang also comes from presence.

JK: Most seekers wonder if someone can be in this presence all the time. They believe one has to be in a constant state of presence in order for the search to be over. But I would say that Liberation has nothing to do with being in a special state all the time. I think that real freedom also includes the freedom to feel identified because the latter is also an expression of Consciousness. Simply because this limitless Consciousness is always available, no matter how we feel or behave. That presence in the background is always there, isn't it?

FL: That which counts is this presence in the background which knows itself. And that is constant at a certain point. The mind becomes simple and the body becomes less tense. But it can seemingly be overshadowed by the appearance of objects, by situations.

JK: That is why I say that people don't have to feel peaceful all the time, because nothing can be excluded. After Liberation, there is still the appearance of feelings, bodily sensations, and so on. For example, if you hit your toe …

FL: It hurts.

JK: You may respond by saying nothing, or shouting or whatever. It doesn't matter any more.

FL: You may use the words you normally don't use.

JK: The real freedom to me is that everything is allowed now, that we don't have to imitate the spiritual idealistic images any more. Otherwise, you are in a golden cage.

FL: I will tell you a story about my teacher [Jean Klein]. You know that I spend a lot of time with him. At one moment he was feeding the fish in his garden. I was standing next to him, and I remember he lost balance and hurt his leg on the concrete border of the pool.

JK (laughing): I can see the picture.

FL: At that moment, he shouted 'merde!' [French for 'shit!']. And he was the kind of person who never used such words.

JK: It was a spontaneous reaction. Nothing is wrong with that.

FL: Maybe the difference is that there is no more psychological suffering. You just do your best, but there is no personal involvement other than a practical one.

JK: Exactly. The appearance of the personal life just goes on, seemingly. The main character still seems to play his role.

FL: You don't become superman!

JK: Yes! And you don't have to. You can behave exactly as you are, because as you are is the divine expression. I suppose that what is done during satsang is that belief systems and concepts are taken away. The taking away of ignorance.

FL: Yes. But there are consequences of falling away from false concepts that go far beyond the psychological area. If I stop thinking about myself as a personal entity, and acting as such, that has psychological consequences. For example, in the way you are perceived by others, and the way you perceive others: that changes. As a result, our interactions also change. Not only your neighbour becomes your friend, but the world becomes your friend. Once you are open to life, it is a miracle.

JK: Yes.

FL: We could also explain this in terms of freedom. You see, there are two kinds of freedom: there is freedom *from* and freedom *to*. The first freedom we encounter on this path is the freedom from the personal, to be free from the personal vision. Free from ignorance. After you encounter this first freedom, you discover the freedom *to*. All the desires we had, they strangely get fulfilled. Because the desire that we don't call upon as a person becomes God's desire, becomes an expression of freedom itself. Beyond any expectations. Desires get fulfilled way beyond that.

JK: There is abundance, but on the other hand there is also this neutrality. A sense of neutrality, of not being involved personally.

FL: Yes. You see, the objects are not desired for themselves, but for the hand that gives them.

JK: The source where it is coming from, is your celebration, in a way.

FL: The desire gets fulfilled only when we are detached from it. And there is the revelation of the divine hand that delivers it.

JK: Then of course, there is not much left to say. Although you may be asked to come to Amsterdam or London to talk about this.

FL: You see, when satsang is taking place, there is nobody giving satsang. The man who is apparently giving satsang is exactly the same as those who are apparently receiving satsang. In other words, the giving hand and the receiving hand are the same.

A mirror reflecting

JK: It is sometimes said that one of the characteristics of your teaching – if I can use that word – is that you don't claim anything for yourself. Is that correct?

UG: It is correct. But 'teaching' is not the right word. Teaching is something you use when you want to bring about a change. And I don't see any need to change anything.

JK: I see.

UG: Philosophers and professors in the university say to me, 'We have so far not been able to create a system of thought from what you are saying.' They also say, 'We can write any book about a philosopher from the past or the present, but what *you* are saying can never be fitted into any frame. We can't create a system of thought about U.G.'

JK: That is why 'teaching' is not the right word.

UG: I am asserting all the time, time and again, that there is nothing there to be changed. So how can you use whatever I am saying to bring about a change.

JK: I see.

UG: I am not interested in freeing anybody from anything. That is my approach. Right from the beginning it is false to suggest one can save anybody.

JK: There is no agenda. No spiritual goal. No spiritual ambitions.

UG: For example, 'You must refrain from selfishness.' Why should anybody be freed from selfishness? Some amount of selfishness is necessary for us to survive in this world.

JK: Yes. Of course.

UG: It is the demand of being unselfish which is creating selfishness.

JK: I see.

UG: I am not in conflict with this society because it cannot be any different from how it is. I don't have any value system, and I don't want to fit into any system. As long as people have a war inside, there will be war outside.

JK: What is it that makes you go and talk around the world?

UG: I am just a dog here, a dog barking. You come here and make the dog bark. You come here asking questions, and I am just a computer. What is coming out of me is something which I don't know.

JK: I see.

UG: There is of course consciousness here [pointing at his body]. I am aware of what is happening around me, and aware of what is going on in my body. Actually, there is no inside and outside. That division is only a thought.

JK: Yes.

UG: It is not that I am mystifying my words, or putting it in a framework of mysticism. What I am saying is so mechanical. It is here [pointing at his body] in this computer, in the data bank or whatever it is called. So, you press some buttons on my computer, and the computer comes out with the answer. There is nothing here [pointing at his body].

JK: I see what you mean.

UG: There is no activity here. And I am not mystifying it, I am just putting it in physiological terms. The brain is a very idiotic thing; it is just a container and a reactor. I am saying so many things. This [pointing at his body] produces so many words. But it does not know what it means. As I told you, *you* are the one who is operating the computer. And when you are asking a question, I am not even listening to the question. There is no listener listening and translating. Both questions and answers are but noise.

JK: All these interviews are completely useless.

UG: Yes! I have nothing to say about anything. I don't know anything. Whatever comes out has been put in it. I am like a shit-box. All that has been put in it is the shit, and whatever is coming out of me is more of shit [laughter]. I am sorry to use such language.

JK: There is no need to say you are sorry.

UG: I know, you are right. Saying I am sorry is just an old habit. Oxford and Cambridge. Education. The Victorian influence.

JK: An old programme.

UG: Anyway, it's as absurd to say that there is somebody thinking, it is even ridiculous to say that there are thoughts. That there is somebody. It is only through the continuous use of memory that we can create a sense of identity.

JK: Yes.

UG: In fact, I never felt really sorry in my entire life. 'Take it or leave it.' Anyway, in this shit-box I don't find any thoughts. There is no such thing as 'thought'. Do we know what thought is? What is thought? I am not asking myself any questions, *others* are asking.

JK: All you are saying has no personal involvement.

UG: Yes. And I am not saying that out of humility. All that I am saying, all the radio interviews, all that has been published in my books, I don't know what I am saying. I am no more than a mirror reflecting.

JK: You have no choice: the words just come out.

UG: Actually, we don't have any freedom of action because all of our action is a reaction.

JK: Yes.

UG: To me, every event is an independent event. It is only afterwards that people look at a series of events and make a story of it. And give it some kind of meaning or importance. If you are trying to change things, it puts you on a merry-go-round: it never stops.

JK: Yes.

UG: I don't believe anything any more. All the spiritual belief systems ... That is not my way of functioning. And I did everything. Everything. I stayed in a cave for seven years. From the age of fourteen to twenty-one. I studied all the books. Every book, every spiritual practice.

JK: Why did you do that?

UG: Because I wanted to be sure that they were all false [laughter]. When I was seventeen and sitting in that cave, I still had a natural drive. I found out that something was wrong. Why? Why should I deny myself? Why can I not go out and reproduce myself and go gracefully? Why deny myself? Why condemn sex? Then I arrived at a point where it was not necessary for me to deny sex. I was twenty-one and in the Theosophical Society and there were girls from all over the world. They were all stuck there because of the war. I was then considered to be a handsome guy. But I didn't go to the other extreme. My question was not about going into sex. I wanted to know why sex was condemned in spiritual life.

JK: I see.

UG: If 'desire' is a hormone, then the whole story about ethics and religious rules is a failure.

JK: Yes.

UG: Once I was giving a lecture in India, in the Theosophical Society. There happened to be a Catholic priest sitting there. He got up and asked me a question about celibacy. And I told him, 'If for any reason you want to be free from sex, you have got to be free from God. I don't know why you are into this celibacy. Get God out of your system and sex will automatically follow. Both of them spring from the same source. Why insist that God is so important? Don't be so serious! Everything is divine.'

JK: So many misunderstandings and interpretations are around.

UG: Oh yes.

JK: Especially regarding spirituality.

UG: Yes.

JK: There are for example a lot of misunderstandings regarding karma and reincarnation.

UG: I remember I was only seven years old when we were attending the golden jubilee of the Theosophical Society. And there were 3,000 delegates from all over the world. And the first time you meet, people introduce themselves and say, 'I was Queen Victoria in my past life, what were you?' or 'I was Alexander the Great in my previous life,' and I found out that there was no historical figure left for me. No spiritual teacher was left for me. What was I in my previous life? Who am I? What was I in my past life? Finished. So from that day on I left all my belief in karma and reincarnation. India was of course the foundation of all this. They always translate those terms like 'karma and reincarnation' in completely the wrong way. There are so many terms translated and copied without knowing what they mean.

JK: What do you mean?

UG: Maya, they say, means 'illusion'. Maya is not illusion. The word 'maya' means 'to measure'. So, whenever you are measuring, there must be a point 'here' [pointing at his eyes]. So there is a relation from this point to the things you measure.

JK: Oh yes, absolutely.

UG: It is the measuring from this point which creates the

illusion. But the world itself is not an illusion. When someone comes with a gun to shoot you, you don't call that an illusion?

JK: Yes.

UG: The way they tried to translate things is so funny. There is no such thing as 'karma' in the usual sense. It is all just response to a stimulus. But response and stimulus cannot be separated. It is one unitary movement.

JK: The law of action and reaction.

UG: Yes! Action and reaction. Nowadays scientists are also saying that the brain is a reactor, that it cannot create anything. The brain doesn't play a major part in this body, it is just a reactor. Physiologists today are now finding out that it is indeed not how it has been described all those years. In the light of their experiments they realized that the brain just plays a minor part in the body.

JK: Really?

UG: All nonsense. Right? It is the human mind. The human mind that makes up everything.

JK: OK.

UG: This morning, I was saying that all the animals are in the highest spiritual state all the sages are talking about.

JK: I see.

UG: No need for spiritual teachings. Don't listen to the holy men. You take it for granted that they are all wise men, that they are spiritually superior to us all, and that they know what they are talking about. Let me tell you: they don't know a damn thing! There are so many saints in the market place, selling all kind of goods. For whatever reason they are doing it, it is not our concern, but they are doing it. They say it is for the welfare of mankind and that they do it out of compassion for mankind and all that kind of thing. All that is bullshit anyway. All the saints or gurus: they don't do themselves what they are saying their followers should do. They say, 'do as I say,' but they are not doing it themselves.

JK: Buddha was not a Buddhist.

UG: Some people come to see me because they believe I have something that they don't. They want something from me. They want something. They want to be at peace with themselves, but all that they are doing to find peace is what is destroying the peace that is already there. All their seeking has led them nowhere. It has all been useless. The living organism is not interested in all the spiritual techniques. When once they have a spiritual experience there will be demand for more and more of the same, and ultimately they will want to be in that state permanently. Talking about bliss, eternal bliss, unconditional love – all of that is romantic poetry. The search is endless.

JK: Oh yes. They will go on searching until they find out that there is no such thing as 'the beyond', no such thing as 'coming home', no such thing as 'the unknown'.

UG: The intention in studying the lives or the biographies of some of those people whom you think were enlightened is to find a clue as to how it happened to them, so you can use whatever technique they used and make the same thing happen to you. That is what you want. And those people give you some spiritual techniques, some methods which don't work at all. They create the hope that some day it will happen to you. But it will never happen. There is one thing that I am emphasizing all the time: it is not because of what you do or what you don't that this kind of thing happens. And why it happens to one individual and not another – there is no answer to that question. I assure you that it is not the man who has prepared himself, or purified himself to be ready to receive that kind of thing. It is the other way around. It hits. But it hits at random. It is like lightning: it hits at random. It strikes at random. It has no cause. All this seriousness about the spiritual goal … Let me tell you that all that wanting leads seekers nowhere.

And I have nothing to give.

JK: No need to get serious about all this.

UG: What is the point of being serious about this subject? We have said enough. It was nice meeting you.

JK: Thank you.

UH: Where are you from?

JK: Belgium.

UG: I love Belgium. I like their chocolate.

This is it

INTERVIEW WITH JAN KERSSCHOT BY KEES
SCHREUDERS, FIRST PUBLISHED IN *AMIGO*[68]

KS: What role have teachers played in your spiritual path, and what is the importance of a teacher for the seeker?

JK: I have had many teachers on the apparent path and each of them has taught me something. Most of them are mentioned in this book. In fact I have unlearned a number of things by meeting the 'real' spiritual teachers. Step by step you let go of a number of convictions till you notice that there is nothing left, including the seeker who hoped to become enlightened some day. Finally you see that the clear presence that you are has never been away.

Tony Parsons was my final teacher – if I can use such words – and I ask myself if it is really necessary to meet a teacher. I think it is different for each seeker. Anyway, meeting Tony was important to me – apparently. The very first time I met him in Hampstead (London) there was a direct resonance when he said, 'This is it.' Those three words dissolved all my questions instantaneously. The conversations we had, the time we spent together, all of that revealed and unmasked all sorts of ego games I used to have.

Nevertheless I want to add here that my testimony might give the reader the idea that there is indeed a process from 'not enlightened' to 'a little enlightened' to 'totally enlightened'. Such a belief in a progressive path is very popular, but according to me it is completely contradictory to what Liberation really is all about. The belief in a spiritual path that leads to the top of the mountain is based on two basic misconceptions: the importance you give to the personal part of the story (how can I reach It?) and the belief that you still nurture in the phenomenon of time, your hope for a better future (when will I reach It?).

As long as you have not understood that Liberation is not personal and that it is timeless, you are like the donkey following a carrot. True Liberation is impersonal, and therefore you can not claim It for yourself. I – as Jan – can never possess It. Moreover, It is timeless (not 'here and now' but beyond time and space), and thus That can never be projected in the future. If you nevertheless do so, you are just fooling yourself – although in the end there is nothing wrong with fooling yourself either. I want to propose that It is not some sort of state of perfection – now or in the future. In fact you can read all that I am saying in other books about this subject. But maybe you will only read what you want to read, and continue to hold onto your misconceptions and belief systems. I notice that some readers of my books manage to succeed in not seeing what I am pointing at.

A true spiritual teacher will point out all these misconceptions to the seeker, until all spiritual ambitions melt away. And I am sure that a direct confrontation with someone who is clear and direct about these things can be very inspiring.

KS: You talk about 'real spiritual teachers'. That implies that there are also 'less real teachers'. What is the difference between these two? Is that the difference between the so-called 'progressive' path (step by step) and the 'direct' path?

JK: Now we encounter a paradox. If you read my book carefully you will see that I often seem to contradict myself. That is inevitable because I have to use words which are dualistic by nature: words cut the unity into parts; words describe things and we take the words for real. But that doesn't work when we are talking about the One. Being one, Liberation, coming home or nonduality are concepts after all. It's best to forget about all these words.

Regarding your question: there are no real versus unreal or less real teachers. Although some teachers I met were in fact misleading their followers, I don't want to criticize the so-called teachers of the progressive path any more. To me, the real teacher is not present as a personality and is in this way a mirror for the seeker − who is in fact also empty. There is nobody there! And in this emptiness they are both one. Then there is no longer any difference between seeker and teacher, between this and that, between Liberated and not Liberated. In other words, there is nobody home.

In my book *Nobody Home* I describe the emptiness as Consciousness, but remember: that word is also just a label. The unlimited Consciousness is indescribable. It cannot be reached, and therefore It can never be projected into a future state of perfection. And It can not be projected into a teacher − no matter how special or inspiring the teacher may be. That is why I always deny that I have reached It. I don't present myself as an enlightened teacher or a realized being, or as someone who tries to open other people's hearts during satsang. I also don't suggest that I can pass It on to others. How can the infinite possibly be passed on? And where are those others if there is only one Consciousness? The only thing that I can do is unmask a number of misconceptions. That seems sufficient to me and I don't need to bring anyone anywhere. I don't see the need for saving anyone. Or bringing the Light to everyone. Or saving the world. For me It is everywhere, so why worry? The Light is equally available in those who say they don't see It. The Light is equally available in the good guys as in the bad guys.

As I said earlier, the progressive path can only exist if we believe in the personal and the temporary. That is why I have described the progressive path as less real because I don't believe in the temporary and the personal any more – except for strictly practical reasons of course. My usual day-to-day life goes on as before, but my spiritual ambition has disappeared. The spiritual materialism I used to have has dissolved. And saying that may be misleading because there is no me who can speak about 'mine'. This 'I' is also just an image appearing in the Light.

And let me remind you that the progressive path is also just another appearance, another image in consciousness. And I am not pointing at the quality or the meaning of the images, but at the Light in the images. I am not interested in all the differences between the spiritual paths, I am not interested in all the differences between the spiritual teachers.

Still I can't say there is really something wrong with the progressive path, just as there is nothing wrong with all other things that appear on the screen. And why is that? The one who judges, the one who criticizes that progressive path, is himself an image that appears. Also the one who – as I just did – dares to suggest that the so-called direct path is superior to the progressive paths, this person is also an image on the screen, and is in fact totally unimportant.

KS: On the progressive path there is hope for the seeker, there is the belief that progress and evolution exist. However, on the direct path there is no seeker and no teaching. Is it true that nothing can be transmitted?

JK: There is nothing that can be transmitted, because what I point to in my books and lectures has no boundaries. No limits in time and space. Therefore It is always and everywhere. Nothing or nobody can ever be excluded from It. I will say it again, nothing or nobody can be excluded! So how could it be possible to transfer It from here to there? From one person to another? Whoever suggests such a transmission or process is talking about something other than the Liberation I am referring to. They are talking about transcendental experiences, the energy of group meditations, spiritual insight, peak experiences, personal growth, a feeling of peace or a sensation of love. These may all be very exciting or interesting, but it is not what my books and talks are all about. As I said repeatedly, there is absolutely nobody home: there is nobody living in the teacher, and there is nobody living in the seeker, so what are we talking about?

KS: Can you tell me what you remember about Jan Kersschot as a seeker? What was his apparent path?

JK: Your questions are becoming more and more difficult because you assume that there was a person who experienced the following story, but it only seems like that. And the funny thing is that it appears real to me, too. I do indeed remember Jan as a seeker, but all those memories are happening right here right now, not ten or twenty years ago. I will play the game of time in order to answer your question. But remember that my personal experiences basically are not important – they are only experiences. I don't want the reader to compare their own experiences with mine. That is exactly what the book *Nobody Home* is not about! There are so many books with personalized stories. There are so many seekers who have become confused or frustrated because they compare their own spiritual experiences with the experiences described by some spiritual hero. It is sometimes quite misleading.

So, Jan was a very serious seeker, passionate but nevertheless very critical. Although I would leave no stone unturned until I had found It, I was convinced that I should not abandon my western life. I felt no need to leave everything behind me in order to go and live in a monastery or ashram. Looking for the One has nothing to do with changing your clothes or accepting a new name. I found that my search had to be compatible with family life, with wine, sex, meat, BMWs, luxurious vacations and all the other things that are usually labelled as unspiritual. Maybe that is one of the characteristics of my search: if I am searching for the One, for the universal, It must be available to everyone at all times, irrespective of behaviour or spiritual practice. That was my point of view and there were not many who shared this vision with me.

If I was really searching for the One, I thought I could not exclude anything. It became clear to me that I didn't give a damn about any spiritual codes of behaviour. Who could impose any rules if my search is all about the universal? As a result, I had to unmask and put in perspective many rules and belief systems, especially the rules of New Age, Christianity, Buddhism and Hinduism.

My transcendental experiences go back to my early youth. One that I remember is when I was fifteen. While kissing, there was suddenly a moment of total openness. You could call it a spiritual experience but that sounds a little too serious, too religious. It was very simple, very childlike but nevertheless very physical. It is hard to talk about it, but I could describe it as pure presence. It was unexpected but so crystal-clear, and at the same time 'I' was not involved in it. Nowadays I wonder if this particular experience may have been the drive for my further so-called spiritual seeking, who knows?

Later on, I started reading about yoga, and I started practising transcendental meditation. During my first meditation I transcended a kind of boundary. I recognized that 'something' waited for me, an indescribable emptiness that also seemed very familiar. It was as if I recognized an old feeling of oneness. It was like meeting an old friend who was more 'me' than my own personality. It was like coming home to the indescribable. It was so familiar at the same time. As I wanted to know more about it, I started reading more. I became a spiritual seeker.

On my (apparent) path I came across all sorts of teachers, some in the form of books (for example Yogananda, J. Krishnamurti, Osho, Da Free John, Sai Baba, Deepak Chopra, Wolter Keers, Margo Anand, Jean Klein, Lao Tze, Alan Watts, Sri Nisargadatta, Ramana Maharshi), others in the form of living teachers or gurus (Armando Acosta, Jacques Lewensztain, Alexander Smit, Andrew Cohen, Ranjit Maharaj, Francis Lucille, Douglas Harding). As I said before, some were inspiring, others rather misleading.

Douglas Harding's experiments especially were a revelation to me. The first time I did the pointing exercise, it was as if the curtains of my 'window' were suddenly cleansed. I think it was in 1995 or '96. Everything that I had read before in all those books now became crystal-clear. It was 'seeing' instead of 'hearsay'. From understanding to *being*. Later on, I had more and more periods of openness, pureness and total emptiness. And although I had the impression of being on the right track, the spiritual hunger was still not satisfied. I read even more books: for example by Justus Kramer Schippers, Eckhart Tolle, Ramesh Balsekar, Wayne Liquorman, Suzanne Segal and Chuck Hillig. Gradually all kinds of belief systems were unmasked. Nevertheless I still had a spiritual path in my head, a future goal, even if I didn't realize it as such. Ego games were still going on somewhere at a very subtle level: comparison, longing, expectations, idealizations, and so on.

On the other hand I felt that I was sitting on a melting iceberg and that the sea I was floating on was getting warmer and warmer. What I didn't yet understand was that I was made of ice myself and that I would finally also melt away. As I still thought that I (as Jan) was on a path to somewhere, I believed I had to make progress on the spiritual path. I was still waiting for an event. Until I met Tony Parsons. During the very first meeting all my expectations evaporated just by hearing these three words, 'This is it'. The idea of there being a path was unmasked, right at the spot. It was like a gentle 'wham'. But this was not some spectacular revelation. No mystical event or anything like that. In a timeless moment, everything became completely clear in a very simple and natural way. The whole house of cards tumbled down, in all simplicity and ordinariness. All questions had disappeared.

And even when (afterwards) the habits of the thinking mind tried to rebuild a house of cards, the illusory aspect of the whole house became absolutely clear. In the beginning it looked as if Tony took away all my hope, until I saw that there never was anyone searching – or for that matter, hoping. So the fan kept turning for a while, even though the plug had already been pulled out. My thinking mind still tried to get things straight, but finally it gave up. Then everything that I still hoped for (in the spiritual field) dropped away. I saw that the seeker I identified myself with had never existed – except as an idea. Sometimes it looked like Tony had me in a hold, but it was actually my own questions I asked him that came back to me like boomerangs. Until it was clear that there is only this. At that time, I also had inspiring conversations with Nathan Gill regarding this subject. He said, 'We are all the very same one.' He made it clear that we are all Consciousness, and that it doesn't matter at all what state you are in. Once that is clear, there is no turning back. When I look at it now, it was as if I found myself in quicksand. But that image is also just an appearance. The death of the ego was actually only the death of an illusion, and therefore not as special as I had always thought it would be. In fact, nothing happened. Everyday life went on. Only the timeless 'This is It' remained.

KS: After 'This is It' – after realizing that you are an expression of Consciousness – has that affected you as a person or as a doctor?

JK: In contrast to what one would expect, Jan and his function in society hasn't changed much. I still have my (apparent) talents and my (apparent) shortcomings. The fact that you have recognized your true nature changes nothing in particular. I could say that I am even less special than before all this happened. Remember: even the one who would have recognized It is an illusion. What I am is Consciousness itself (and so is the reader) and the person Jan appears in this same Consciousness. But I have absolutely no spiritual task or anything like that. I don't see anything that should be changed. I can't see any border between right and wrong. Everything is just as it is. The person known as 'Jan' (and as I said before: that is also an image) may still appear for practical reasons, and that is completely OK.

Nevertheless, there is something that has changed. The need for judging and criticizing is over. There is no fight any more on the spiritual level. The seeking has stopped because the so-called seeker is now recognized as being no more than a concept. Consciousness was there all the time – even when it was not recognized as such. As a result of this insight I cannot claim anything for myself, not even the so-called spiritual experiences that I just described. The 'I' who thought he experienced It was illusory from the very beginning. Even though the experiences were very important for my spiritual ego, now it seems as if they have not happened. It all means absolutely nothing, and that is not some sort of false modesty. They are only images that appear now, that appear in the timeless. They are like memories of experiences in which 'me' was not present. So, how do I dare to talk about it? Anyway, the unity (the One) was there even before the transcendental experiences, during the experiences and afterwards. The One is also present for one hundred percent during those moments that we label as banal, or as unspiritual. When you see that, where should you go?

Interview for *Watkins Review* with Jan Kersschot

BY VIJAY RANA AND JASON BRETT SERLE, FEBRUARY 2003

W: Could you start by telling us a little bit about your book *Nobody Home* and how it relates to your first book, *Coming Home*.

JK: I started writing *Coming Home* first. I started to write a few pages after meeting Douglas Harding, way back in 1995. And as new insights kept on coming, I continued to write them down. But it took me several years before it really became the book it is today. The book developed through meeting so many other interesting people in the following years, like Tony Parsons, Mira, Francis Lucille, Wayne Liquorman and Nathan Gill. I also got a lot of inspiration through the writings of Chuck Hillig, Alan Watts, Ramesh Balsekar, Ramana Maharshi, Nisargadatta, to name a few. All the insight I shared with these people, all the experiences I had, all the belief systems I have seen through, all of that is what has made the book *Coming Home* what it is. I published it in Belgium in 2001.

The book *Nobody Home* is published in the UK by Watkins

and is a shorter, revised version of *Coming Home*. For example, it does not contain the eight interviews in *Coming Home*. But the core of the message is equally there, maybe even more accessible to some readers because the book is only 192 pages instead of more than 400 pages. It contains a few new elements, but basically it is still approaching the subject in the same way as my first book.[69]

W: So, what effect have the meetings with these 'enlightened' people had on you?

JK: It is all about recognition. The recognition of what you really are. That is what can happen when you meet such people. The recognition of the core and essence of your very Beingness. And what is this Beingness? It is the essence of what I am. It is That which cannot be expressed in words. And although it sounds as if I attained this seeing, that is not the case really. I didn't find It, it is rather that It found me.

My first important meeting was the encounter with Douglas Harding. He and Catherine – his French wife – were visiting Belgium about seven or eight years ago. His so-called experiments confirmed what he says in his books: one goes from 'hear say' into 'look see'. The 'clear seeing' was instantaneous, unexpected, mind blowing and still ordinary and obvious. Before, my life was divided into a spiritual life (meditation, reading books) and a profane life (working, eating, sleeping). After meeting Douglas, that distinction was completely gone. I saw that all such divisions are conceptual. Everyday life became meditation. Later on, I visited Douglas on a retreat in France; that is when the idea of the book *Coming Home* came up. He also stayed in my house in Belgium once and he gave a workshop for some friends of mine. Only a few of my friends saw what this seeing was all about, and I was disappointed that most of them didn't value what Douglas was saying. Anyway, for me, this 'seeing' became a natural thing, not something one experiences during workshops or satsangs. I didn't need his experiments any more.

But I also noted some sort of conceptualism in his theory, because he says, 'There is a face over there, and no-face here.' That is of course inescapable if you want to explain these things in a workshop or a book. But it was clear to me that this separation between 'no face' and 'face' was also artificial.[70] One day, I realized that the no-face 'here' encompasses everything, including that face over there. In my books, I describe it as vision X (the human vision) and vision Y (the impersonal vision). Vision Y is the infinite one, and as such encompasses vision X.

A few years later, I met Tony Parsons in Hampstead, London. When I first saw him, he just said, 'This is it.' Maybe it was the way he said it, maybe it was the way I was listening to his words, but it left me with … nothing. In that timeless moment, all my questions were blown away. And with it, the concept of being a seeker. The mask – that was already discovered as being a mask before meeting Tony – now was seen as completely illusory. There was no way back. The roles we play in life are like clothes you put on: you need them to play the game, but they are not what you are.

Tony also made me see that there was no need to wait for a major transcendental event, some sort of mystical experience that I would need to allow myself to stop the spiritual search. I saw Tony several times, during his talks and in private conversations, both in London and in Amsterdam. I also had very interesting conversations with his wife, Claire. The recognition of 'naked Beingness' became inescapable. Waiting for an event, or comparing yourself with some spiritual hero, all these games the seekers play, all of that was seen through. After that, the mind still seemed to try some old tricks to get me back in the game of time and space. But all of those games were unmasked at the spot; my conversations with Tony (and with Nathan Gill) made all of that clear. Then it was obvious that there is nowhere to go, nothing to attain whatsoever. There was no way back, indeed.

I have to add here that I already saw 'That' at the age of fifteen, but at that time I was too young to realize what it was that was seen. One could say that it took me twenty-five years of searching, reading books and meeting all sorts of people to really see that. Well, it was not me seeing it, of course; words can get confusing here. And the funny thing about all this is that the Beingness itself is always the same. What I really am has never been away. I just looked the other way, and that is why I though It wasn't there. The pure Beingness had never left me, and never will.

W: In order to realize Vision Y, it appears that there is a gradual process of development. Prominent authors such as Ken Wilber acknowledge enlightened nondual awareness as the ground of all being but he also acknowledges that *development* plays an essential part in the realization of all that is. What is your view?

JK: Let me start by saying that vision Y cannot be realized. I didn't realize vision Y. And never will. Full stop. I am sure both of you know this, but I just want to make sure that the reader of my book is not going to personalize vision Y. That is a major trick of the seeker's mind, to try and understand vision Y. Or work it out in some way. And vision Y cannot be understood, nor realized by anyone. And why is that? Simply because it is what we are.

In the book *Nobody Home* I explain how vision X is only a limited part of vision Y. I know that this division is artificial, but to a certain extent it can be useful for the reader to make certain things clear. Vision X is the personality we identify with and vision Y is the limitless awareness. As human beings, vision X stands for our *human* part and vision Y for the *Being* part.

But the latter is not a part, but That in which all these ideas and concepts are appearing. It must be clear that the seeker can never attain or realize this Beingness, although that may be interpreted as such when reading about it in my book.

You are right when you say that there appears to be a gradual process of development. And I would emphasize the word 'appears'. Indeed, it appears to ripen in time. But you know that all of these are again concepts: the ideas of 'ripening' or 'development in time' can only appear when our mind starts to compare one condition with another one. But That which I am pointing at in the book, cannot ripen or develop. It just is. And that is timeless. A timeless snapshot. So, the One Beingness cannot develop or change, although it appears to change and develop.

On the other hand, I understand that some authors acknowledge that *development* plays an essential part in the realization of all that is. But that is only true from the limited point of view of the person (vision X). The clarity and ripening can go through some apparent evolution indeed, not the Beingness itself.

I could say that my view on this subject has ripened over the last ten years, yes. But that is again a personal point of view, Jan's view if you like. Again, it is but a concept. And that has nothing to do with Beingness. You see, as I said before, I didn't attain anything special, I didn't realize vision Y. I just lost (seem to have lost) some belief systems. I can say that along with that a certain clarity and understanding appeared. The Beingness itself has never been away, even when I was identified with my role as a spiritual seeker. I didn't come closer to Beingness during my spiritual search. Even when I turned my back to 'what is' my true nature was available one hundred percent. Beingness does not care if it is recognized by Jan or not. Or if Jan can spread the message through his books or talks.

It is only the spiritual seeker who is concerned about personal development, and that may go on until it is seen that the seeker is a concept too. Once this game is seen through, the whole idea about development and spiritual growth becomes ridiculous. There are no more spiritual motives, there is nothing to go for or to work on. The whole house of cards comes tumbling down. Where should you go to find your true nature, if that is what you are?

Last Friday, I was in London to present the book in Watkins, and after the talk there were some questions and answers. I remember that there was a lady asking me how she could continue the glimpse she had of Oneness. She felt as if she saw 'it' and then lost it. I told her that her question felt to me as if she was like water, saying to me, 'I feel so dry'. How can water become wet? I told her that she was already as wet as she could possibly be, although she didn't realize it as such at that moment. How can water ever be 'not wet', how can you ever not be your true nature? How can you ever not be what you are?

Epilogue

When we simply live in recognition of our true nature as Beingness, the need to search for personal enlightenment dissolves into 'seeing life as it is'. Not your life, not my life, but simply 'life'. Seeing that leaves us with no knowledge about ourselves at all. We simply let everything emerge, without trying to stay fixed with one thing, without asking why? or how?, without trying to influence what is appearing. It is about recognizing the divine in the ordinary. It is so fresh and alive that it can never be turned into a system or a method. There are no edges to this Being. This Is-ness cannot be packaged and spread by a religious organization. It is already available: It has always been here. And somewhere we all already see that 'this is it' although we don't necessarily acknowledge it.

Awakening unmasks the belief in a personal agenda. Our personal programme, our trying to get It, our attempts to let go the ego, all of them are expressions of our spiritual materialism. Having an agenda gives the seeker a good way of postponing 'what is', it buys us some time, gives us some personal space to continue to believe in our individual daydream. The mind wants security, wants a goal, hopes for a better future. The personality wants to get rid of its problems. But Beingness is seeing without wanting anything back. It is the end of spiritual business. It is the recognition by nothingness that what we think we are – a personality – is only a ghost. If the person we think we are is but a concept, where should it go? If it is but a phantom, how could it become enlightened?

It is not that we have to get rid of all our individual characteristics and concepts, but we release the investment and the belief in them. We lose interest in the continual chatter of the mind about past and future, about high and low, and so on. All the concepts and beliefs on the spiritual level fall away on their own because they lack our interest. The incredible joke is that we can't possibly avoid our true nature, because we can't run away from what we *are*. Such an Awakening is not an achievement but simply the realization of what one is anyway. The unbounded aware Space, which gives rise to whatever it is that is happening.

What dies is self-importance on a spiritual level. The story of a personality who needs to go somewhere to attain something higher loses its significance completely. The person who wants to prove something, either to himself or others, has been checkmated. There is no place for spiritual pride and arrogance because it is clear now that everybody is equally an expression of 'It'. Aware of forms, we are formless; aware of colour, we are colourless; aware of time we are timeless. This is the One appearing as many, the Subject appearing as objects, the Impersonal appearing as the personal.

This is the end of division and comparison, the end of any form of hierarchy. This is also the end of ownership and the beginning of total poverty. The end of owning feelings, the end of trying to be in control, the end of trying to be holy, the end of wanting to know all the answers, the end of the spiritual search. This is the poverty Christ was referring to when he said that it is more difficult for a rich man to enter the Kingdom of Heaven than for a camel to pass through the eye of a needle. As long as we own our hopes and fears, as long as we own our choice and pride, as long as we identify with our meaningful life story, we are too rich to enter the Kingdom. All our questions and devotion are selfish. Real poverty is not about selling our belongings, leaving our family, taking a new name or living as an ascetic in the Himalayas, it is a matter of unmasking the source of all possessions, which is the sense of 'me'. When it is seen that there is no 'me', the Kingdom of Heaven becomes apparent and includes everyone.[71]

Maybe you picked up this book hoping that it may prepare you for enlightenment. Maybe in my story there were some points of recognition that may have given you hope you might get the same. By now, I suppose you know it doesn't work like that. You know that you don't have to follow me or anyone else. Although most of us seem to come into this subject with the intention of filling a lack, with the hope of getting something, some of us seem to realize that there is nothing to get. Asking how?, when? or why? is not going to unmask the games you play. All that I can tell you is that the seeker you believe you are is but a concept and has no relevance when it comes to Awakening. So this book is not about getting anything, it is about unmasking the seeker. As a result, this book is not addressing you as a separate person: it is addressed to you as Beingness.

By now you understand that I can't give you anything because there is no 'you' I could give it to. Maybe I can take away a few things, although even that is not necessary or recommended. While reading this book, you may have lost a few old conditionings and belief systems. Maybe you have put into perspective the belief in being a separate identity. Maybe you also lost the idea that you have to lose anything. And if you haven't lost any beliefs or concepts while reading this book, if you apparently prefer to hold on to your concepts, that is equally OK because that is also an expression of Oneness.

Notes

1 See also: Kersschot J, *Nobody Home*, Watkins, 2003, pp. 148–153
2 Using a capital throughout may irritate some readers and suggest that Beingness with a capital is separate from the other words which are written without a capital. But Beingness is limitless which means that the words written without a capital are equally included within this Beingness.
3 How could it matter if the spiritual seeker is an illusion?
4 Here again we have to add that the 'you' who is apparently back in the horse race is a phantom, and so is the you who believes you are enlightened. So in the end it doesn't matter. Awakening has nothing to do with *you*.
5 For the ego, 'personal' experiences are very important. They confirm the sense of separation. Just as in an opera by Puccini or Verdi, a lot of attention is given to the personal aspects of life and the dramatic elements of all these emotions and experiences.
6 What you think you are is the actor in the movie, the main character who is trying to turn 'your' life into a good story. Maybe the story is illustrated with flashbacks relating to your history or with a voice-over of a reporter (your inner voice) commenting on what you did and making plans for 'your' future.
7 See also interview with Tony Parsons
8 It is the most popular concept around, and very practical indeed for organizing everyday life.
9 See also: Balsekar R, *The Final Understanding*, Watkins, 2002 p. 79
10 See also: Kersschot J, *Nobody Home*, Watkins, 2003, chapter 2
11 Throughout the book, I will continue to use capitals for those concepts which point to what is infinite.
12 See also: Kersschot J, *Nobody Home*, Watkins, 2003, pp. 148–149
13 Related to this time frame is the law of cause and effect, the law of karma, and so on.
14 This doesn't mean that now we have to believe what this book postulates. If we accept everything without questioning, we create just another belief system. This text doesn't present a new

belief system but describes another point of view that unmasks a lot of common concepts. And it is up to the reader to check its reliability and validity. Don't accept what is said in this book on authority. Finally, everything that is written here is made of concepts, too.

[15] This idea is not very popular, because a lot of people would then feel as if their life had no meaning.

[16] If we said that the north pole is 'good' and the south pole is 'bad', then working for a better world would be like saying 'I want a globe with a north pole but not with a south pole'.

[17] Where is 'your' personality while reading these words? It only appears when you think about it or someone else points you to it. Or when someone describes how you look. Again, those are thoughts, concepts in the minds of you or someone else which appear now and then as images in 'your' movie.

[18] How can we be sure that things must be as they are? Simply because things *are* as they are. It's about recognizing the divine Is-ness of what is. And 'what is' includes everything that appears, including that which we usually don't describe as divine.

[19] The movie is supposed to look real, isn't it?

[20] Both the sleeping dream and the waking dream seem to be real to the dreamer and the daydreamer respectively.

[21] See also: Kersschot J, *Nobody Home*, Watkins, 2003, pp. 36–58

[22] The distinction between the adult personality on the one hand and naked (unidentified) Beingness on the other is of course also a game of the mind. The border between them is purely conceptual, and in a way suggesting there is a step from identification to non-identification is also misleading. There are no steps to Oneness, there is no path to Beingness.

[23] See for example: Tony Parsons, *All There Is*, Open Secret, 2003

[24] They are based on the three belief systems we discussed before: the separation between me and others, between past and a future, and between good and evil.

[25] There are wonderful books that illustrate all these stories, and make them look even more real. There are churches, temples and cathedrals all over the world where you can actually hear and see all these 'important' stories.

[26] This doesn't mean that 'being in wonder at what is' is the new reference, or that 'being childlike' is a new tool to bring you to enlightenment.

[27] It is true that such a description doesn't make sense. As said

before, words are concepts and any book (including this one) about nondualism will always be confusing and full of paradoxes.

[28] See also: Nathan Gill, *Clarity*, G.O.B. Publications, 2000

[29] In other words: there are no guarantees about what our ghost will be like.

[30] The ghost loses its white sheet, and all that is left is emptiness.

[31] There are many books around which describe such spiritual heroes, for example, *Autobiography of a Yogi*, Paramahansa Yogananda, 1946

[32] See also: Chuck Hillig, *Enlightenment For Beginners*, Black Dot Publications, 1999

[33] What we call individuals walking around on this planet is in fact the manifestation of Unicity playing diversity. All the actors are different masks of the same Face.

[34] Both the beach and 'our' sandcastle and the 'other' sandcastles are made of the same grains of sand. Similarly, we are all made of atoms.

[35] Even the word 'misleading' is misleading, because who is there to mislead? Misleading may also suggest that there is 'leading,' and leading means there is a goal or a path to something that must be true, to something higher or better.

[36] See also the experiments in: Kersschot J, *Nobody Home*, Watkins, 2003, pp. 127–132

[37] The mind can't turn dualism into nondualism, but *it doesn't have to* because dualism is only an appearance. There was never any real separation or paper that was cut into two – both the scissors and the separation are fiction, so there is no need to join because the split was only apparent. As a result, all methods that suggest bringing the pieces back together only strengthen the belief in the (illusory) division.

[38] The separation between true and untrue is also illusory. In the end, there is no such thing as 'the final truth', despite the beautiful books that suggest so.

[39] The separation between dualism and nondualism is also illusory, because the first is part of the second and the borderline between the two is purely conceptual. This is illustrated in the drawing on p. 21 of *Nobody Home*, Watkins, 2003

[40] See also: Tony Parsons, *As It Is*, Open Secret, 2000, p. 35

[41] See also: Paula Marvelly, *The Teachers of One*, Watkins, 2002

[42] The word 'misleading' doesn't mean that something is wrong

with them. Even a misleading teacher can't take away Beingness. Whatever 'we' do or believe is an expression of the Light.

[43] The question is then who is going to decide to do that? Where is that person who will switch his perception?

[44] See also: Tony Parsons, *All There Is*, Open Secret, 2003

[45] And 'us' is again another concept appearing in the same Oneness, just like 'you' and 'me' and 'the world' are concepts of the mind.

[46] We can pretend to stop looking for liberation because we heard about a famous teacher who said that enlightenment is the end of the seeking process. So we stop looking for enlightenment, although we still feel a sense of lack inside.

[47] Even the gurus who claim to talk about nondualism while it is obvious that they are leading their followers up the garden path are equally an expression of Oneness. I can't criticize them for apparently misleading their followers for what is the point of one ghost criticizing another ghost?

[48] The sense of being a person, of being the centre of the world, is all a pretence, and that doesn't mean that there is something wrong with it.

[49] Dividing people into daydreamers on the one hand and those rare ones who have unmasked the daydream on the other hand is in fact again a subtle form of dualism. To Beingness, all these divisions don't matter at all.

[50] I don't consider the confusing teachers as 'lower' than the teachers who are clear about this.

[51] See also: www.theopensecret.com

[52] Pointing one's finger to the face and 'seeing' that it points to nothingness, to pure awareness, is one of Douglas' experiments. See also: Douglas Harding, *To Be and Not to Be*, Watkins, 2002

[53] Similar experiments are described in: *Nobody Home*, Watkins, 2003, chapter 4

[54] When it is clear that there is no spiritual seeker, the need to practise disappears.

[55] The first book *Coming Home* (Inspiration, 2001) is sold out and replaced by *Nobody Home*. See also: www.kersschot.com

[56] This is often described as 'the seeker is the sought' because both are illusory and as such equal. There is neither the cognized thing nor the cognizer, there is only the (apparent) cognizing.

[57] The book *Coming Home* was published in Belgium (April 2001)

and is not available any more. Here, Nathan is referring to a text he received before its publication.

58 It was cut later.

59 Wayne Liquorman Acceptance of What Is, Advaita Press, California, 2000

60 Wayne Liquorman, *Acceptance of What Is*, Advaita Press, California, 2000, p. 74

61 See also: http://www.blackdotpubs.com/

62 See also: Hartong L, *Awakening to the Dream*, Trafford, 2001

63 *No Way*, © copyright Advaita Press, California, 1999

64 Liquorman W, *Acceptance of What Is*, Advaita Press, California, 2000, pp. 59-60

65 www.puresilence.org

66 See also: *Nobody Home*, Watkins, 2003, pp. 19-24

67 Tolle E: *The Power of Now, A Guide to Spiritual Enlightenment* Hodder & Stoughton, 2001

68 *Amigo* (ezine n°5): see also : http://www.ods.nl/am1gos/am1gos5/index.html

69 See also: www.kersschot.com

70 See also: Harding D, *To Be and not to Be*, Watkins, 2002 p. 10

71 This means that even those who are too rich to enter the Kingdom of Heaven are still 'included' – even when they still believe they aren't. In other words: there is no passage through the eye of the needle, there is no path from outside to inside, there is no gate to Heaven.